Heart of Conviction

Heart of Conviction
by Tyler Frick

ISBN-13: 978-1732448698
ISBN-10: 1732448698

Copyright © 2018 Tyler Frick

Published by:
Lazarus Tribe Media, LLC
Rome, Georgia

Edited by Rachel Newman

All rights reserved. No part of this book may be reproduced or transmitted in any form by any means, electronic, mechanical, photocopy, recording or other without the prior written permission of the publisher.

Scripture quotations are from The ESV® Bible (The Holy Bible, English Standard Version®), copyright © 2001 by Crossway, a publishing ministry of Good News Publishers. Used by permission. All rights reserved.

Printed in the United States of America.

Publisher's Site: www.lazarustribemedia.com
Author's Page: www.lazarustribemedia.com/tylerfrick

Author's Site: bit.ly/thekingscompany

Heart of Conviction

Tyler Frick

THE KING'S COMPANY

Lazarus Tribe Media
Rome, Georgia

Table of Contents

Introduction	7
1 | Becoming a New Creation	11
2 | A New Father	21
3 | A New Spirit	31
4 | A New Knowledge of Truth	43
5 | Becoming Like Christ	49
6 | Imagine for a Moment	63
7 | Living from the Kingdom	71
8 | Jesus as Messiah	85
9 | The Quickening Spirit	99
10 | Jesus as King	117
11 | Warring Under the King	139
12 | Jesus as Lord	149
13 | "I'm waiting for my people to trust my position."	159
14 | "I'm ready for my people to trust my perspective."	173
15 | "I'm ready for my people to join me on my vineyard venture."	185
16 | Laying Down Sin	193
17 | Confirming God's Presence	205
18 | Conviction in Fellowship	209
19 | Soundness of Faith	213

Introduction

Blindness is a condition of the body that becomes less burdensome as one's surroundings become more understood and a sense of direction is established. In fact, the fear of the unknown can vanish from daily life when it is no longer the center of mental identity. Without acquiring the knowledge of what actually exists around us, the fear of what is unknown will tend to overpower our ability to find rest. Awareness of what might exist beyond our personal borders helps to diminish that fear and causes us to remain confident in our current positions.

We exist in a physical state of flesh surrounded by sound, light, and structures. We gain experiences and memories every day that help us to cope with what we see unfolding from moment to moment. Those of us who can see with our physical eyes are able to detect physical threats such as moving cars or uneven foundations in our paths with plenty of time to avoid encountering them, under the condition that we remain observant. If we remain observant, we might see what we need to avoid, as well as what we might need to embrace.

What I want to shed light on in this book, however, is not our ability to observe that which exists in the physical realm, but something even more valuable to our lives. My objective is to provide biblical understanding of the importance of spiritual awareness. It is to explain the reality of the spiritual realm that exists with us, that we are unable to see physically, but that we must inevitably encounter on a daily basis, moment by moment.

What takes place in the spiritual realm affects us more abruptly than we might think. Actually, there is so much happening around us in the spiritual relam, that our minds can't even contain it all at once. Our thoughts, feelings, and choices are dependent on spiritual influence whether we recognize it or not. Because of our minds' dependencies on spiritual influences, we live in a constant state of war. In this war, we are not the soldiers, we are not the weapons, we

Introduction

are the battlefields. The forces of darkness and the presence of light are each contending for dominion over our souls. That is, they are warring for dominion in our minds, wills, and emotions.

Believe it or not, we are able to recognize the status of the war taking place over every life. We can recognize who has gained dominion by observing our speech, our thoughts, and our character. If a blind man looks into a mirror, he is wasting his time, because he cannot see the image produced in the reflection. On the other hand, a man who has received his sight is made able to recognize and observe the image he bears. In this life, we must become aware of the image we bear, we must choose to receive sight so that we can more fully understand the driving forces behind our identities. Becoming aware of how the world experiences us is the path we must take in leading us out of our ignorance, and into a knowledge of what truly exists around us, upon us, and what exists within us.

Spiritual blindness has become contagious in the people of the world. Instead of pursuing spiritual life, spiritual truth, and spiritual holiness, people in all nations seek the passions of their flesh. Because of this, righteousness is not prevalent in society. Morality is at one of the lowest points it has ever been across the globe. Not only do we see blatant disregard for the things of God in the personal lives of millions, but we also see it in the governmental systems of the world.

Fear, worry, and anxiety seem to be the driving forces in most economies. As a result, nations flood their wealth into research, discovery, war, and healthcare, all while seemingly neglecting issues like broken families, hunger, and homelessness. The reason why these things have taken precedence over people, is due to the influence of spiritual warfare. For us to become effective in reaching these lost souls scattered across the planet, we need to understand the truth about the workings of the spiritual realm, and come to know God personally. Without his help, we will never be equipped to overcome the destruction of society that we must inevitably face.

If you would like to know more about The King's Company, including personal spiritual development opportunities, visit:

bit.ly/thekingscompany

Or, visit the author on Facebook at:

www.facebook.com/pastortylerfrick

1
Becoming a New Creation

"But, as it is written, "What no eye has seen, nor ear heard, nor the heart of man imagined, what God has prepared for those who love him"— these things God has revealed to us through the Spirit. For the Spirit searches everything, even the depths of God. For who knows a person's thoughts except the spirit of that person, which is in him? So also no one comprehends the thoughts of God except the Spirit of God. Now we have received not the spirit of the world, but the Spirit who is from God, that we might understand the things freely given us by God. And we impart this in words not taught by human wisdom but taught by the Spirit, interpreting spiritual truths to those who are spiritual." 1 Corinthians 2:9-13 ESV

In the above passage, we learn that God has revealed his own thoughts to us through the Spirit, who searches all things, even the deep things of God. The word here in this verse, "revealed," holds an interesting verb tense that does not exist in the English language, but in Greek, represents the absence of any particular moment in time. This is called the "aorist" verb tense. When an "aorist" Greek verb tense is used, it does not represent past, present, or future tense. In this particular passage, the word is "aorist active indicative." That tells us that at no specific time, the Spirit did reveal to "us" (each individual person who loves God) the thoughts of God.

Now, because revelation occurs within one's own mind, bringing to fruition the fullness of a realized thought, we should recognize that these thoughts we are destined to receive will occur separate from another person's mind. One cannot receive a revelation within his own mind, and instantly, another person receives that exact same revelation at the same time, unless it is the Holy Spirit revealing to each one individually through himself, at the same time! The Holy Spirit is able to influence the mind of a man so that the thoughts of God are deposited on the inside of him. Of course, the existence of a thought alone is of no value unless it is put to work. It must be weighed and applied according to the recipient's will in the matter.

God has not chosen to reveal his thoughts to only a few, but to

Chapter 1

all who would become his adopted sons or daughters. He desires to reveal his own thoughts to each of his children, through the Spirit, as an ongoing deposit of his fullness, so that we might make continual withdrawals from the treasures placed in our hearts, in turn manifesting his identity and image in the physical realm we currently live in. This is that which was promised, the gift of entering into a relationship with the person of the Holy Spirit.

The Holy Spirit can be thought of as God's intercessor, sent to plead the cause of the Father to the minds of his children. Just as Jesus intercedes to the Father on our behalf, the Holy Spirit intercedes to us on the Father's behalf. He reveals to us the thoughts of God, after all, he is the one who knows those thoughts which have been given freely to us through adoption.

By learning to hear the voice of the Spirit, we are made able to abide in his love, and in Christ. We are made able to bear the image of our Father as representatives in his kingdom. To get a fuller understanding of how this new image we are able to bear might manifest in our lives, we will need to take a look at another passage.

"And calling the crowd to him with his disciples, he said to them, "If anyone would come after me, let him deny himself and take up his cross and follow me. For whoever would save his life will lose it, but whoever loses his life for my sake and the gospel's

will save it. For what does it profit a man to gain the whole world and forfeit his soul? For whoever is ashamed of me and of my words in this adulterous and sinful generation, of him will the Son of Man also be ashamed when he comes in the glory of his Father with the holy angels." Mark 8:34-36, 38 ESV

Through the provisions Christ made on the earth, all of the knowledge and wisdom existing in God's eternal state of existence has been made readily available to us. It manifests in our minds as we choose to deny our former selves and receive grace from moment to moment in our new states of existence. Our new self, the new creations we have become in and through Christ, must act obediently by denying our old selves, so that the lives we see in reflection are a direct representation of the new image we have been given to bear.

Inside of every born-again Christian, there exists two "selves," the new and the old. The old self is meant to be buried with Christ, but far too many who seek to enter the kingdom don't understand that the old self is not buried until the choice has been made to deny it. That choice is not made by the Holy Spirit, or by Christ himself. The choice to bury the old man can only be made by the new man. The new self must choose to deny the old self, so that one might be able to live as the new man, without the sinful desires and passions we experienced in our former absence of knowledge.

Chapter 1

This is why we should all experience water baptism. In the process of water baptism, we make public professions of our new-found faith in Christ. We then are buried under the water in full submersion as a prophetic representation of enduring Christ's death with him on the cross, and in the grave. When we rise from the water, we are prophesying resurrection life over ourselves in a beautiful picture of what it is like to enter into newness of life in Christ.

The new creation we become is governed by three things.

A new Father,

A new Spirit,

A new knowledge of truth.

Formerly, we were born of sin, into sin, fathered by the lies of the kingdom of darkness. Our spirits, although our own, were born cursed by the sins of our ancestors and of our fathers. This may seem drastic and far-fetched to some, to recognize the kingdom of darkness as our immediate spiritual influence at the time of physical birth, but it is true. In fact, the knowledge we are born into is the knowledge belonging to the world of sin, death, and destruction. It is not until we receive new life that we encounter the Spirit of adoption as sons and daughters of God, at which time we receive the regeneration of the Holy Spirit, along with the reception of the fullness of the knowledge of truth, belonging to the kingdom of God. When we are born again into the kingdom of God, we experience an exchange of fatherhood. Our old spiritual guardianship is put behind us and a new relationship with the God of Abraham, Isaac, and Jacob is experienced.

At the time we receive this new life, we meet the Spirit of adoption, gaining a Father in God, and experiencing the truth which abides in our new family bloodline. This is of course a spiritual bloodline, by which all men who receive Christ are saved. There is no other way to eternal life than through Jesus, and his blood.

> *"Now there was a man of the Pharisees named Nicodemus, a ruler of the Jews. This man came to Jesus by night and said to him, "Rabbi, we know that you are a teacher come from God, for no one can do these signs that you do unless God is with him." Jesus answered him, "Truly, truly, I say to you, unless one is born again he cannot see the kingdom of God." Nicodemus said to him, "How can a man be born when he is old? Can he enter a second time into his mother's womb and be born?" Jesus answered, "Truly, truly, I say to you, unless one is born of water and the Spirit, he cannot enter the kingdom of God. That which is born of the flesh is flesh, and that which is born of the Spirit is spirit. Do not marvel that I said to you, 'You must be born again.' The wind blows where it wishes, and you hear its sound, but you do not know where it comes from or where it goes. So it is with*

Chapter 1

everyone who is born of the Spirit." John 3:1-8 ESV

All people experience a natural, unspiritual, baptism of flesh. It does not have any spiritual significance in it other than the prophetic revelation that might be received through observing it. Before natural birth occurs, babies are knit together in fluid. We are fully immersed in fluid in our mother's womb. Just before birth, a mother's water will break, and after that comes the birth of a baby.

Before the baby ever breathes its first breath, it experiences a natural baptism of water. After that, we are each immersed in air and breath our first breath. The same happens when we embrace the spiritual baptisms of water and Spirit. Water baptism is the physical baptism, and the receptions of the outpoured and in-breathed Holy Spirit are the spiritual. Not to say that one must occur before the other, but that the natural choice to be washed must be made in recognition and acceptance of the Gospel, and with that, the new man receives the in-breathed and out-poured Spirit of God in recognition of Christ's resurrection life and the necessity of being endued with power from on high by the gift of the Holy Spirit.

The above passage reads, "..You must be born again.' The wind blows where it wishes, and you hear its sound, but you do not know where it comes from or where it goes. So it is with everyone who is born of the Spirit...." Where it says, "the wind blows where it wishes," the literal Greek translation says, "the spirit spirits where it desires," or "the spirit breathes where is wishes." By looking further into this passage in Greek, it goes on to say that we will indeed hear the sound of uttered words in the speech of a tongue! Therefore, when we are each born of Spirit, we will each hear a sound of uttered speech in a tongue! This does not merely suggest the reception of the gift of speaking in tongues, but rather the ability to receive the voice of the Spirit and relay his words in our speech, whether in known or unknown tongues. We will first hear his uttered speech in our hearts, and through that reception, we will be empowered to speak from God's heart to others. This manifested voice of the Holy Spirit in our lives is the sure result of being baptized in Spirit!

Jesus was speaking to Nicodemus about receiving the gift of the Holy Spirit, and being made able to perceive the thoughts of God through the Spirit, who reveals the heart of the Father, moment by moment, in an understandable, internal language. This aspect of the presence of the kingdom is vitally important to understand to begin living in the newness of life that we receive through Christ. Without believing that we can hear the voice of the Spirit, we cannot live in the fullness of new life. We have to yield to his voice to be led by his Spirit, and those who are led by his Spirit are the children of God.

Chapter 1

"For those who live according to the flesh set their minds on the things of the flesh, but those who live according to the Spirit set their minds on the things of the Spirit. For to set the mind on the flesh is death, but to set the mind on the Spirit is life and peace. For the mind that is set on the flesh is hostile to God, for it does not submit to God's law; indeed, it cannot. Those who are in the flesh cannot please God. You, however, are not in the flesh but in the Spirit, if in fact the Spirit of God dwells in you. Anyone who does not have the Spirit of Christ does not belong to him. But if Christ is in you, although the body is dead because of sin, the Spirit is life because of righteousness. If the Spirit of him who raised Jesus from the dead dwells in you, he who raised Christ Jesus from the dead will also give life to your mortal bodies through his Spirit who dwells in you. So then, brothers, we are debtors, not to the flesh, to live according to the flesh. For if you live according to the flesh you will die, but if by the Spirit you put to death the deeds of the body, you will live. For all who are led by the Spirit of God are sons of God. For you did not receive the spirit of slavery to fall back into fear, but you have received the Spirit of adoption as sons, by whom we cry, "Abba! Father!" The Spirit himself bears witness with our spirit that we are children of God, and if children, then heirs—heirs of God and fellow heirs with Christ, provided we suffer with him in order that we may also be glorified with him." Romans 8:5-17 ESV

Because we are privileged to be led by God's Spirit throughout our earthly lives, we need to understand practically how to hear and apply that leading in a mature manner. There is no need to act socially awkward as a result of being led by the most Holy Spirit. There is, however, a need to act holy.

I mentioned that as we become new creations through regeneration, we receive three new things.

A new Father

A new Spirit

A new knowledge of truth.

Let's take a look at each of these, in the light of living in our new lives, as new creations. First, I must mention that the receptions of these are to be received initially, and perpetually. There is an initial reception of each, as well as an ongoing reception. It is not mature to suggest that a simple moment of acceptance or reception of any of these three provisions is enough to sustain a holy lifestyle. Instead, we will need to experience continual relationships with each.

2
A New Father

As I mentioned previously, before entering into new life in Christ, we lived in an unhealthy state of illegitimacy by which we were born into sin and governed by the spiritual nature of the kingdom of darkness. This produced in us the immediate focuses of self-preservation. Instead of relying on God for our protection and security, we carried the burdens of life on our own shoulders. We fought for survival in life by considering that we were capable of achieving rest by our own means.

We all lived for ourselves, sacrificing for ourselves, fighting for our own personal desires at the expense of others. We all demanded attention and unhealthy gratification. Even at the early stages of childhood, we took things into our own hands, as if we were able to meet our own needs! As young toddlers, we fought, kicking and screaming, crying and biting to have things go our own way. We were all focused on getting our own way, and we all failed miserably as we grew older. In keeping with our selfish tendencies, we fought for some idea of self-induced inner peace that could never be reached, hurting many others along the way. Have we not all walked the path of selfishness in an effort to gain the world? If so, have we consequently experienced a pursuit that ends with losing our souls?

Why were selfishness, envy, and pride, along with other negative characteristics, so instinctive? Some better questions reveal the truth about those destructive lifestyles we chased.

Who fathered those destructive lifestyles? Who put those behaviors inside of our hearts from the beginning?

To better understand this, we need to look at another Greek word. There are a couple different words for "father" in the Greek language, but I want to dissect the word "*pater.*" From this word, we get the words "paternal" or "parent" in the English language.

The word "*pater*" is both literal and metaphorical in definition. In its most literal sense, it describes a generator or ancestor, both male or female. It portrays the parent to be the one who produced the corporeal nature of the offspring. It can be used to describe both immediate ancestors or even more remote ancestors, such as the founders of a tribe or people group, that is, the forerunner of a people, such as Abraham, Jacob, or David. Pater can even be used to suggest the ancestral influence of forefathers, or fathers of nations.

Metaphorically, it can be used to recognize an originator and transmitter of anything. For example, some recognize the original pastor of a church congregation to be a "father" of the church, or a "spiritual father" to the people within the congregation, based primarily on their influence in the beginning of the ministry. Sometimes we encounter people in our lives who serve us as parents would, training us up in the ways they think we should go. Paul fathered Timothy in the faith, training him in righteous and holy living just as Jesus taught the disciples. Therefore, Paul was considered to be a spiritual father to Timothy.

Also, in continuing on the metaphorical usage of this word, it can be used to identify authors of societies of persons. Today, we might call someone a "father of a movement," such as Martin Luther King Jr. or other reformers like the father to the protestant movement, Martin Luther. We could even consider George Washington to be one of the fathers of America. In such cases, the disciples of movements which overtake societies, who walk in these fathers' and mothers' footsteps, have chosen to become active under the same spiritual influences as those figures. Every movement that has ever taken place on the earth has been rooted in some spiritual ideology. Likewise, there are more deliberate uses of the word "pater," which describe one who has infused his own spirit into others for the purpose of actuating and governing their minds. In this case, the spirit is given a fuller control, a more welcomed influence by the mind(s) of the offspring.

We can look at this in two lights. First, we should recognize the ability Christians have to hear the thoughts of God internally by the Spirit who has been welcomed to influence and govern the mind by the choice one makes to receive the Spirit from our heavenly Father. Negatively, some have given influence to demons, or evil spirits, in order to be able to give unhealthy and spiritually corrupt power or information to others, such as necromancers, mediums, soothsayers, or spiritists. These people have chosen to allow evil spiritual influence to actuate and govern their thoughts, so that they might gain financial or economic advantages through occult practices, as well as other returns beyond finances.

In the same way, we all have the opportunity to open ourselves up to the leadership of ministers in the Church, so that we may receive healthy spiritual teachings or prophecies for our lives. In these

Chapter 2

cases, we open ourselves up to be the recipients of spiritual truths, and by doing so, allow our minds to be influenced by the words of leaders speaking from their Christ-given seats of influence. However, we must be sure that we submit to those who have been appointed by Christ, and who remain in him. Not all who profess Christ actually lead from a place of personal intimacy with him. This is one reason why we have so many denominational doctrines, which many firmly believe to be accurate, yet vary and differ throughout the church.

We can see it throughout the world today. There are thousands of churches, and somewhere around forty thousand "denominations" currently practicing faith. Obviously, they are not all in unity in doctrinal beliefs, but claim to serve the same Lord. If that were true, would not all of these believers agree on doctrine, having received the same Spirit from God? Therefore, we must be sure that what we are being taught bears witness with the Holy Spirit at work in our lives. We should never come under the teaching of anyone who is in opposition with the Holy Spirit.

In continuing, God is called the Father of the stars, the heavenly luminaries, because he is their creator, upholder, and ruler. By this we know that the universe itself, along with all of creation, is subject to the authoritative influence of his voice. He is the Father of all rational and intelligent beings, whether they be angels or men, because he is their creator, preserver, guardian and protector; that is, if they remain subject to him, recognizing him as such. Every person has been given the option to choose to be fathered by God, and although he is their creator, many reject him as their ongoing protector and preserver. By doing so, they are laying themselves open and bare, vulnerable to illegitimate spiritual and physical fathering.

This is why all who seek eternal security must, by faith, choose to become sons and daughters of God. He is the Father of those who, through Christ, have been exalted to an especially close and intimate relationship with him, and who no longer dread him as a stern judge of sinners, but revere him as their reconciled and loving Father.

He is the Father of Jesus Christ, who has been united with the Father since the beginning in the closest bond of love and intimacy. Christ acquainted himself with the Father's purposes, and was appointed to explain and carry out among men the Gospel, the plan of salvation. In this way, he established the only way to share also in his own divine nature. By receiving Christ, and being joined to him, we also are given to share in the Father's divine nature, bearing his image and his likeness. The requirement for this relationship is faith!

Now, in consideration of what has been read so far regarding the Greek word "*pater*," let's revisit at an earlier consideration:

Chapter 2

"Why were selfishness, envy, and pride along with other negative characteristics so instinctive? A better question reveals the answer. Who fathered those destructive lifestyles? Who put those traits inside of our hearts from the beginning?"

This perspective of fathering can help us to understand some radically offensive biblical teachings, such as we read in 1 John.

"Everyone who makes a practice of sinning also practices lawlessness; sin is lawlessness. You know that he appeared in order to take away sins, and in him there is no sin. No one who abides in him keeps on sinning; no one who keeps on sinning has either seen him or known him. Little children, let no one deceive you. Whoever practices righteousness is righteous, as he is righteous. Whoever makes a practice of sinning is of the devil, for the devil has been sinning from the beginning. The reason the Son of God appeared was to destroy the works of the devil. No one born of God makes a practice of sinning, for God's seed abides in him, and he cannot keep on sinning because he has been born of God. By this it is evident who are the children of God, and who are the children of the devil: whoever does not practice righteousness is not of God, nor is the one who does not love his brother." 1 John 3:4-10 ESV

The purpose of this passage is to cause us to want to consider the "father" of every one of our thoughts. When we find ourselves caught in the busyness of our minds we should ask, "Am I thinking maturely? Am I thinking holy or destructive thoughts?" It is crucial that we understand how every one of our thought patterns might eventually create helpful or destructive physical, emotional, or spiritual action. For instance, thought patterns rooted and grounded in love may result in actions taken in love, such as serving someone else joyfully. On the other hand, destructive thought patterns founded on immature thinking may result in actions taken out of bitterness or hate, which could result in a multitude of negative consequences.

If we realize that our thoughts are destructive, can we pinpoint the influence of those thoughts? The answer is, Yes! Not only can we uncover unhealthy root systems in our thinking, but if after believing in Christ for the first time we are continually filled with Holy convictions from the Spirit that intend to curb our emotions and desires toward a more Christ-centered existence, we can begin to abandon these destructive mental strategies by learning to rest in the power and freedom that belongs to the children of God!

When we enter into newness of life through faith in Christ Jesus, we receive a new Father, the Father of lights. Where light abounds, darkness must flee! When the holy thoughts of God consume our minds, what is unclean is forced to vacate! As Christians, our focus should never be on sin, but on the Father who exposes sin. By allowing God to father our thoughts, we are allowing the most Holy spiritual influence to govern and actuate our minds! When God begins to author our thoughts, we begin living the destinies he writes on our hearts and minds. As his chosen and adopted sons and daughters, we receive a covering that protects us as we develop into images of love.

3
A New Spirit

Just as we have received a new Father, we also receive a new Spirit. His name is Holy, and he regenerates us in order that we too might become holy. The Holy Spirit is the Spirit of adoption, who joins us together with God the Father and Christ in Spirit. He has been poured out on all flesh in order that the children of God might be joined to the Father in heaven. Because he has been sent, we have the opportunity to be filled with him and clothed in his power, in order that we might receive the provisions of the kingdom of God in our lives in many different ways. Initially, we are filled with his presence so that we might receive a revelation of the reality of our adoption, and that revelation is the first of many inner witnesses that take place in our hearts.

> *"If you love me, you will keep my commandments. And I will ask the Father, and he will give you another Helper, to be with you forever, even the Spirit of truth, whom the world cannot receive, because it neither sees him nor knows him. You know him, for he dwells with you and will be in you. "I will not leave you as orphans; I will come to you. Yet a little while and the world will see me no more, but you will see me. Because I live, you also will live. In that day you will know that I am in my Father, and you in me, and I in you. Whoever has my commandments and keeps them, he it is who loves me. And he who loves me will be loved by my Father, and I will love him and manifest myself to him." Judas (not Iscariot) said to him, "Lord, how is it that you will manifest yourself to us, and not to the world?" Jesus answered him, "If anyone loves me, he will keep my word, and my Father will love him, and we will come to him and make our home with him. Whoever does not love me does not keep my words. And the word that you hear is not mine but the Father's who sent me. "These things I have spoken to you while I am still with you. But the Helper, the Holy Spirit, whom the Father will send in my name, he will teach you all things and bring to your remembrance all that I have said to you. Peace I leave with you; my peace I give to you. Not as the world gives do I give to you. Let not your hearts be troubled, neither let them be afraid." John 14:15-27 ESV*

Jesus told the disciples that he would not leave them as orphans.

Chapter 3

What did he mean by that? By this time, they had already been baptized in water, and had placed their faith in Jesus as their Messiah. Why did Jesus address them as orphans? The Greek word used here, "*orphanos*," can describe someone who is without parents, but it can also describe one who is without a teacher, guide, or a guardian. When Jesus walked with them, he protected them on many occasions with the power and authority that he carried. In John 6, Jesus fed five-thousand with two fish and five loaves of bread.

> *"Now the Passover, the feast of the Jews, was at hand. Lifting up his eyes, then, and seeing that a large crowd was coming toward him, Jesus said to Philip, 'Where are we to buy bread, so that these people may eat?' He said this to test him, for he himself knew what he would do. Philip answered him, "Two hundred denarii[a] worth of bread would not be enough for each of them to get a little." One of his disciples, Andrew, Simon Peter's brother, said to him, "There is a boy here who has five barley loaves and two fish, but what are they for so many?" Jesus said, "Have the people sit down." Now there was much grass in the place. So the men sat down, about five thousand in number. Jesus then took the loaves, and when he had given thanks, he distributed them to those who were seated. So also the fish, as much as they wanted. And when they had eaten their fill, he told his disciples, 'Gather up the leftover fragments, that nothing may be lost.'" John 6:4-12 ESV*

In Matthew 8, Jesus spoke peace to a violent storm, sparing the frightened disciples from the ferocious waves.

> *"And when he got into the boat, his disciples followed him. And behold, there arose a great storm on the sea, so that the boat was being swamped by the waves; but he was asleep. And they went and woke him, saying, "Save us, Lord; we are perishing." And he said to them, "Why are you afraid, O you of little faith?" Then he rose and rebuked the winds and the sea, and there was a great calm. And the men marveled, saying, "What sort of man is this, that even winds and sea obey him?""" Matthew 8:23-27 ESV*

In Matthew 17, Jesus sent Peter to catch a fish which held a coin in its mouth in order that they might pay their taxes.

> *"When they came to Capernaum, the collectors of the two-drachma tax went up to Peter and said, "Does your teacher not pay the tax?" He said, "Yes." And when he came into the house, Jesus spoke to him first, saying, "What do you think, Simon? From whom do kings of the earth take toll or tax? From their sons or from others?" And when he said, "From others," Jesus said to him, "Then the sons are free. However, not to give offense to them, go to the sea and cast a hook and take the first fish that comes up, and when you open its mouth you will find a shekel. Take that and give it to them for me and for yourself." Matthew 17:24-27 ESV*

While he was with them, he taught them about faith, but also assisted them when they were lacking it by performing these types of signs. When Jesus ascended, the disciples were without a personal guardian, teacher, and guide with whom they could speak to and learn from. Without this type of help, they would be orphans in that sense. Nevertheless, when the Holy Spirit came, he fulfilled their need for the presence of a helper.

When we think about who the Holy Spirit is, and what he has been sent to do, we need to realize that he was first sent to adopt the orphans. As a minister, I love how the Holy Spirit manifests himself through me during times of ministry in order to touch other's lives. I believe he came to do that, to work through us as we remain obedient and submissive as "willing" vessels for God's glory. Yet, before he works through us, he works in us. In order for him to work in us, we have to recognize him as more than an energy source. Unfortunately, many who believe in Jesus do not recognize the Holy Spirit as a person, but rather a "power source." He is much more than that! The Word clearly defines his roles and personalities all throughout Scripture.

One of the most interesting (and most overlooked) roles that the Holy Spirit plays in our lives is that of a parent. I think that too often we don't allow him to speak to us as a parent, a teacher, a guide, or even a guardian, but he wants to. Christians are obviously not perfect in how we come to make every decision, but the Holy Spirit is willing to make us holy and righteous in all of our ways if we will listen to him and be obedient to what he tells us.

So many of us still struggle inwardly with hidden sins, addictions, or regrets. It would be a lie for me to say that we are all completely pure in our hearts and minds, and although the Father looks at us and sees Christ, we don't always look in the mirror and see him ourselves. Most of us tend to struggle internally with our own perception of our identities. I think that is normal, but we shouldn't rely on our own thoughts alone when we are personally analyzing ourselves. It would be so much more powerful if we would all seek God's perspective of our identities by listening to the voice of the Holy Spirit. We need to be honest with our feelings and emotions within ourselves, but even more so in our communication with God.

I can think back to a day when I was struggling pretty badly internally, turning against myself in spirit, and wrestling with God in my desires. I had sinned against him in an area where I had felt that I already received freedom, and my weakness broke me. I remember, I was crying out to God in the midst of my shame, and I realized that the reason for my sin was birthed from an absence of love for God. At least that's what it felt like inside. I remember saying, "Why don't I love you! Why did I love sin more than you!," and as I wept, broken

Chapter 3

in shame, the Holy Spirit began to speak something to me.

I saw words being written on a wall in my mind's eye, as if I was watching a video in my imagination. The words kept coming into place out of nowhere, piece by piece. They read,

> *"You are still in love with your old sin nature, but grace has been given for you to hate it. Your old life can't stand in the presence of your new life, and so it is trying to push your new life away. Your new self has been forgiving him for the struggle and has been allowing him to remain close. Stop giving grace to what I have set you apart from. Deny your former ways, and love God."*

In that moment, I realized what I had been doing. I had allowed an unhealthy understanding of grace cause me to think that my old way of life was acceptable because Christ had given his life for it. Somewhere in my mind I had clung to a lie that told me Christ saw value in my old life, and that's why he paid for it on the cross. That is a lie! Jesus did not find value in my old life, but in my new one! I had never chosen to reject what I thought Christ died for. What I hadn't understood was that Jesus didn't die on behalf my old man, so that he might live. He died to crucify my old man, so that by being raised from death I might walk in his resurrection life. He died to give me new life, and in order to receive it, I needed to walk like him, talk like him, and act like him in every way! He gave himself up for me so that I might be empowered by grace to push away my old nature, and receive newness of life.

By receiving that teaching from the Holy Spirit, who was working to protect me, guide me, and guard me from evil, I was able to understand the real root issue that was causing me to sin. The problem wasn't that I didn't love God, it was that I didn't hate the sins that destroyed me in my former way of life before I met Christ! The Holy Spirit was teaching me, disciplining me like any good parent would, so that I would grow up and mature in the way that he desires for me to walk!

Imagine if I didn't listen for the teaching of the Holy Spirit in my time of struggle. I would still, to this day, be lost in a lack of knowledge that he rooted out that day in order to protect me from harm. I might still be giving grace to my former self. I might still think that Christ gave grace to my old man instead of recognizing that grace was given to my new man, so that I could deny my old way of life, my old sin nature.

This type of help from the Spirit is available to every born-again believer who has received the Spirit who is from God! His voice can come in many different forms, such as correction, encouragement, teaching, or even power. However he speaks, it is always out of love. When we receive newness of life, we receive a new Spirit, the Spirit of truth! He becomes our new teacher, guide, counselor, helper, advocate, and guardian! Because the Spirit has been sent to help us in life, we are able to become slaves to Christ, putting to death our old sin nature, and living in the freedom of a relationship with God. The new law at work in our members, then, is the law of the Spirit, which is the law that, in itself, contains freedom from shame and condemnation. The voice of the Holy Spirit turns our struggles into shouts, and our mourning into laughter!

> *"Likewise, my brothers, you also have died to the law through the body of Christ, so that you may belong to another, to him who has been raised from the dead, in order that we may bear fruit for God. For while we were living in the flesh, our sinful passions, aroused by the law, were at work in our members to bear fruit for death. But now we are released from the law, having died to that which held us captive, so that we serve in the new way of the Spirit and not in the old way of the written code." Romans 7:4-6 ESV*

If we allow our old character, which died with Christ, to rise up again in our thought lives, we are subject to shame and fear. We would be choosing to battle against a nature that never will change. Through the guardianship of the Spirit, we become lovers of God's values, living in peace and perfect harmony with his mind. That is not to say that we will not struggle. Actually, we will indeed suffer for Christ if we truly love him. We will be persecuted and rejected for his name. Yet, by the grace given to us in the Holy Spirit, we will be able to overcome anything that comes against us. The reason this is true is because the Holy Spirit's favorite thing to do is to teach us how to love Jesus more.

"You then, my child, be strengthened by the grace that is in Christ Jesus, and what you have heard from me in the presence of many witnesses entrust to faithful men, who will be able to teach others also. Share in suffering as a good soldier of Christ Jesus. No soldier gets entangled in civilian pursuits, since his aim is to please the one who enlisted him. An athlete is not crowned unless he competes according to the rules. It is the hard-working farmer who ought to have the first share of the crops. Think over what I say, for the Lord will give you understanding in everything.

Remember Jesus Christ, risen from the dead, the offspring of David, as preached in my gospel, for which I am suffering, bound with chains as a criminal. But the word of God is not bound!" 2 Timothy 2:1-9 ESV

"Only let your manner of life be worthy of the gospel of Christ, so that whether I come and see you or am absent, I may hear of you that you are standing firm in one spirit, with one mind striving side by side for the faith of the gospel, and not

frightened in anything by your opponents. This is a clear sign to them of their destruction, but of your salvation, and that from God. For it has been granted to you that for the sake of Christ you should not only believe in him but also suffer for his sake, engaged in the same conflict that you saw I had and now hear that I still have." Philippians 1:27-30 ESV

"Beloved, do not be surprised at the fiery trial when it comes upon you to test you, as though something strange were happening to you. But rejoice insofar as you share Christ's sufferings, that you may also rejoice and be glad when his glory is revealed. If you are insulted for the name of Christ, you are blessed, because the Spirit of glory and of God rests upon you. But let none of you suffer as a murderer or a thief or an evildoer or as a meddler. Yet if anyone suffers as a Christian, let him not be ashamed, but let him glorify God in that name. For it is time for judgment to begin at the household of God; and if it begins with us, what will be the outcome for those who do not obey the gospel of God? And, "If the righteous is scarcely saved, what will become of the ungodly and the sinner?" Therefore let those who suffer according to God's will entrust their souls to a faithful Creator while doing good." 1 Peter 4:12-19 ESV

4
A New Knowledge of Truth

There is a type of knowledge belonging to the world, a knowledge of both good and evil, that produces worldly fruit if it is ever relied upon. It is sometimes referred to as "the knowledge of man" in Christian circles. We were all born into this world without knowledge. Yet, shortly after our births, our minds get bombarded with the knowledge of man, whether we were born in Christian homes or not. Throughout our childhood, we encountered all types of people, many of whom influenced us with the world's knowledge, and in turn, led us to believe things about ourselves that are not consistent with the knowledge of God. We need to know and appreciate that not all knowledge is good. Remember that in the Garden of Eden the tree that Adam and Eve were told not to eat from was the tree of the knowledge of good and evil. When they chose to eat of that fruit, their spiritual lives were changed. They may have gained knowledge, but by doing so, they also gained death.

When we become followers of Christ, we immediately receive a new knowledge of truth by faith. That new knowledge is not the knowledge of this world, but the knowledge of God, who is not of this world. Whenever it is received, it immediately begins to plow through the soil of our hearts. Because we are surrounded by the knowledge of man, our hearts have been sown with bad seeds. They are the lies we had previously been told which we received as good knowledge. They produced inconsistencies in our characters, causing us to live in opposition with God's predetermined will for our lives. This new knowledge of truth, that which is from God, begins working in power when we first accept it in order to heal our misunderstandings of truth. It is supernatural at its core.

The new knowledge is the good news, the message of the Gospel of Christ. Every born-again believer must believe that Jesus was sent by the Father into the world to live a sinless life, die on a cross, and be raised from the dead in order to restore what man had lost in the Garden of Eden. Again, this revelation of truth is supernatural at its core, therefore it must be received by faith. It cannot be received by mere intellect or logical reasoning because it is not something we can see with our own eyes. This new truth we receive becomes the basis for understanding newness of life, and every ounce of knowledge gained from the foundation of the Gospel must agree with its message, otherwise it is false.

By receiving this new knowledge, an entirely new world of possibilities is made available to Christians, in accordance with each one's individual faith. Even though Christians receive a new Father and are joined to him by the Holy Spirit, each one must progress in knowledge as our faith is being perfected. From the time we first believe, and continuously as we remain in Christ, we are given measures of faith as gifts from God. As we each receive our own measures of faith, we must also share in the faith of others so that our knowledge is made full.

"I thank my God always when I remember you in my prayers, because I hear of your love and of the faith that you have toward the Lord Jesus and for all the saints, and I pray that the sharing of your faith may become effective for the full knowledge of every good thing that is in us for the sake of Christ." Philemon 1:4-6 ESV

Each one if us receives our own measure of faith by which we are empowered to believe. It is a duty of Christians to share the various details of our faith with other believers so that we might all grow together in unity. Unity is more fully achieved when we believe together! Therefore, we should never become discouraged when we recognize a larger measure of faith in others, but should join ourselves to them in hopes that we might be able to believe for more by sharing with them in what they have received by the same Spirit who is also at work within them.

> *"For by the grace given to me I say to everyone among you not to think of himself more highly than he ought to think, but to think with sober judgment, each according to the measure of faith that God has assigned." Romans 12:3 ESV*

I mention this aspect of faith because it is our faith that strengthens our knowledge. In fact, it works both ways. Just as our faith works to increase us in knowledge, so also our knowledge works to increase faith. They are a dynamic duo in Christian life. Faith comes to us when we hear the words of God, either from Scripture, by the voice of the Spirit, or by listening to each other. As we hear truth from those sources, knowledge and faith abound in love to cover us with perfect comfort as we await the coming of our Lord.

> *"For the Lord gives wisdom; from his mouth come knowledge and understanding; he stores up sound wisdom for the upright; he is a shield to those who walk in integrity, guarding the paths of justice and watching over the way of his saints. Then you will*

understand righteousness and justice and equity, every good path; for wisdom will come into your heart, and knowledge will be pleasant to your soul; discretion will watch over you, understanding will guard you..." Proverbs 2:6-11 ESV

One of the most beautiful realities of the Christian life is that we are, together, members of a growing family. Not only do we have the opportunity to live in relationship with God, but we are also privileged to spend time with each other. We are called to not only commune with God in Spirit, but to embrace fellowship with our Christian brothers and sisters in the same Spirit, that by doing so, we might each increase and abound in love for God and for one another.

Without attaining unity in the faith regarding what we believe to be true, we will never be able to operate as one body. The Gospel of Christ is the knowledge we attain by faith that not only serves to help us identify Jesus, but is also that which networks Christians all over the world together as one body. Without the reality of one, true Gospel message, we could all claim allegiance to God and his kingdom, but never be able to agree on the person of Christ Jesus. Therefore, by our own lack of knowledge, we would remain dead in our trespasses and sins, and never attain salvation. Jesus is the only way to salvation, and the message of his life, death, burial, and resurrection is the power unto salvation. Therefore, we must be sure that the Gospel we have received is not one that has been tampered with or changed in any way. False gospels are present throughout the world. We must never allow them to become convincing to the point that we come into agreement with them in our minds. With the pure knowledge of who Jesus is and what he has done for us, we can identify and cast away any inconsistency presented to lead us astray.

5
Becoming Like Christ

"So Jesus said to them, "Truly, truly, I say to you, unless you eat the flesh of the Son of Man and drink his blood, you have no life in you. Whoever feeds on my flesh and drinks my blood has eternal life, and I will raise him up on the last day. For my flesh is true food, and my blood is true drink. Whoever feeds on my flesh and drinks my blood abides in me, and I in him. As the living Father sent me, and I live because of the Father, so whoever feeds on me, he also will live because of me. This is the bread that came down from heaven, not like the bread the fathers ate, and died. Whoever feeds on this bread will live forever." John 6:53-58 ESV

I used to think that abiding in Christ had to do with refraining from sin. I thought not abiding in Christ meant that I was sinning, or that I was somehow unclean in God's eyes. I do believe that living outside of sin has a part to play in it, but living pure is actually a result of abiding, not the prerequisite for it.

Abiding in Christ is what produces a noticeable change in lifestyle, but it is not a physical act. In fact, whether or not someone abides in Christ is not visible to the naked eye. That's because the realm of abiding is soulish. It is a condition of the mind, will, emotions, and character. It is not physical, nor is it solely spiritual, but is an expression of the condition of a man found within the relationship he has between the Spirit and body. More practically, it is a condition of the heart.

When we are in Christ, his identity is recognized through us by spiritual and physical expressions such as speech or patience. The fruit of the Spirit are identifiers of our inner condition in Christ, as are the actions and words we release from our lips. Without these types of expressions, the condition of one's heart is not able to be realized.

When we choose to abide in Christ, we are not only striving to live pure, but we are seeking to be in agreement with God's heart. Jesus did nothing apart from the Father's heart, and likewise, we can

Chapter 5

do nothing of value in the kingdom apart from Christ.

> *"So Jesus said to them, "Truly, truly, I say to you, the Son can do nothing of his own accord, but only what he sees the Father doing. For whatever the Father does, that the Son does likewise. For the Father loves the Son and shows him all that he himself is doing. And greater works than these will he show him, so that you may marvel. For as the Father raises the dead and gives them life, so also the Son gives life to whom he will. The Father judges no one, but has given all judgment to the Son, that all may honor the Son, just as they honor the Father. Whoever does not honor the Son does not honor the Father who sent him. Truly, truly, I say to you, whoever hears my word and believes him who sent me has eternal life. He does not come into judgment, but has passed from death to life." John 5:19-24 ESV*

Jesus not only lived on the earth so that he could model a lifestyle worthy of following, but also asked the Father to send the Holy Spirit to speak to us, not in his own accord, but only what he is given to speak.

> *"When the Spirit of truth comes, he will guide you into all the truth, for he will not speak on his own authority, but whatever he hears he will speak, and he will declare to you the things that are to come. He will glorify me, for he will take what is mine and declare it to you. All that the Father has is mine; therefore I said that he will take what is mine and declare it to you." John 16:13-15 ESV*

This tells us that in the same way Jesus was able to see and understand what the Father was doing, we too can follow his lead because of the help of the Holy Spirit. We can each learn to do what God is doing because we can receive the Holy Spirit who speaks to us from God's heart! Everything he speaks comes directly from Jesus. This is also why those who abide in Christ can receive whatever they pray for because they only pray for what they hear God wants.

If I were abiding and remaining in Christ, and God spoke to me through the Spirit that I was to preach the gospel in Africa, I could pray in faith for it to occur, and it would indeed come to pass. So, we must ask the Holy Spirit this question: "What does the Father want me to do?" To be walking in obedience to the things that are revealed to us through the Spirit is to be abiding in Christ. In this aspect of abiding, sin becomes a distant cousin, irrelevant to the ongoing growth and development that comes from remaining in Christ.

When it comes to bearing the image of God, living in his likeness, having the mind of Christ that is free from disorder, and being led by the Spirit, we should want to have some practical directions to follow for understanding how to do it. It's one thing to know how we've been called to live, but it's another to know how to do it. Funny thing is, the answer has been right under our noses the entire time. The key to learning how to continually live in these powerful conditions

Chapter 5

is communion.

> *"For I received from the Lord what I also delivered to you, that the Lord Jesus on the night when he was betrayed took bread, and when he had given thanks, he broke it, and said, "This is my body which is for you. Do this in remembrance of me." In the same way also he took the cup, after supper, saying, "This cup is the new covenant in my blood. Do this, as often as you drink it, in remembrance of me." For as often as you eat this bread and drink the cup, you proclaim the Lord's death until he comes. Whoever, therefore, eats the bread or drinks the cup of the Lord in an unworthy manner will be guilty concerning the body and blood of the Lord. Let a person examine himself, then, and so eat of the bread and drink of the cup. For anyone who eats and drinks without discerning the body eats and drinks judgment on himself. That is why many of you are weak and ill, and some have died. But if we judged ourselves truly, we would not be judged. But when we are judged by the Lord, we are disciplined so that we may not be condemned along with the world." 1 Corinthians 11:23-32 ESV*

Why would God urge us to continue in taking the Lord's supper? Could it be that we are called to follow religious practices when we meet? No. Communion is not about taking the bread and wine as a religious practice. Taking the Lord's supper is about remembering.

How do you suppose the church at Corinth could remember

what Jesus had done? Were they present throughout his life or on the day he was sacrificed? Did they each see him on the cross? No, and that's not the point at all. I want to break a small piece of this scripture down for us, so that we might be able to understand the purpose of partaking in the Lord's supper in a more meaningful and practical way. I want us to understand how we are able to continue bearing God's image and remain in Christ.

> *"...and when he had given thanks, he broke it, and said, "This is my body which is for you. Do this in remembrance of me." In the same way also he took the cup, after supper, saying, "This cup is the new covenant in my blood. Do this, as often as you drink it, in remembrance of me." 1 Corinthians 11:24-25 ESV*

First, we need to understand what the body is. The word used in Greek in verse 24 for "body" is "*soma.*" It means just that, a body, but what is interesting is that Jesus was not speaking of his earthly body. He spoke of his heavenly body that would later be raised from the dead. It does not represent the body before it was broken, or while it was broken on the cross, but the body which had been saved and brought up from the grave! In fact, the root word for "*soma*" is "*sozo,*" which we know now to mean "healed, saved, delivered." Jesus did not break up his old body to be shared among the church, but his new body, that the church might receive a taste of resurrection!

Chapter 5

When Jesus broke bread with the disciples, it was a prophetic act that would be further understood in the days following their meal.

Jesus said, "Do this in remembrance of me." We need to look into this word, because we who are alive today have no explicit memories of Jesus living on the earth. We only have the ability to remember what we know of him from the testimony of witnesses, which we have in the New Testament.

Is that what we are supposed to be thinking of here? Are we to think of his sacrifice, his earthly ministry, or his resurrection? The Greek word for remembrance is "*anamnesis,*" and is described as a recollection. Again, at face value we would assume this means that we should be recollecting from memories of Jesus, but the root words tell another story. The first two roots for this word are, first, "*ana*" which means "in the midst of," and the second "*mimneskomai,*" which means to return to one's mind. Already we see something taking place that is apart from simply remembering.

With the knowledge of these root words, we can begin to understand that by doing this in remembrance, we are re-entering or returning to our new mind in Christ. If someone were to lose a member of their body, such as an arm, and it were reattached, that would be a re-membering of their body. When we think about taking communion in remembrance of Jesus, we should think about being rejoined to him as a member of the body.

When we break *mimneskomai* down, we find that it has two very interesting base root words. The first is "*meno*" means "to remain or abide," in reference to a state or condition. For our particular study, it is to remain in one mind, not to allow our minds to become different than Christ's. The other root word is almost comical. It is "*masaomai*," which means to chew, consume, eat, or devour!

We must understand that Christ Jesus had broken the bread to represent his sharing amongst the church of his own resurrection nature, so that we might be joined to him in his body. He exhorted the brothers in his command to continue doing so by remaining in one mind with Christ, not straying from the one mind, but abiding in it so as to remain one in his body!

When we take part in the physical act of communion, the Lord's supper, we do so in order to return to the mind of Christ, and remain solid in our identity as his body! That's one reason why Jesus said in John 6:

"As the living Father sent me, and I live because of the Father, so whoever feeds on me, he also will live because of me. This is the bread that came down from heaven, not like the bread the fathers ate, and died. Whoever feeds on this bread will live

Chapter 5

forever." John 6:57-58 ESV

The physical act of communion works like an ignition. Once the mind is focused on Christ, we need to continue focusing on him. Keeping our focus on Christ and his kingdom is an act of the will, which is part of our soul nature. When we do this, the Spirit is able to speak to us more easily, and we are able to be led by him.

In my opinion, taking communion with our families, friends, or congregations is the best way to choose together, in harmony, to follow Christ. We take part in the physical act, which restores and refreshes our souls, allowing the Holy Spirit to influence us with less resistance. When we abide in Christ, we welcome the Holy Spirit's voice. When we choose to do things our own way, we are resisting his guardianship.

Next, we will look into what it means to partake of the "cup."

"In the same way also he took the cup, after supper, saying, "This cup is the new covenant in my blood. Do this, as often as you drink it, in remembrance of me." 1 Corinthians 11:25 ESV

The Greek word for cup in this verse is *"poterion,"* which holds both literal and metaphorical meaning. The literal meaning describes a vessel, such as a physical cup that we would drink out of. Metaphorically, it can be used to represent one's experience, whether joyous or adverse, such as favorable or unfavorable divine appointments, which are likened to a cup which God presents for one to drink. We might call it "one's lot in life."

All of us have been allotted a time for physical birth, which was not by choice, but a cup nonetheless. In considering both meanings of this word, we should consider that the cup taken in communion is not our own. Jesus said, "This cup is the new covenant of my blood," therefore it is not our own lot being received, but Christ's.

Jesus blood contains the elements of his soul, just like our blood contains the elements of our souls. Isaiah 53 tells us that Christ poured out his soul unto death.

> "Yet it was the will of the Lord to crush him; he has put him to grief; when his soul makes an offering for guilt, he shall see his offspring; he shall prolong his days; the will of the Lord shall prosper in his hand. Out of the anguish of his soul he shall see and be satisfied; by his knowledge shall the righteous one, my servant, make many to be accounted righteous, and he shall bear their iniquities. Therefore I will divide him a portion with the many, and he shall divide the spoil with the strong, because he poured out his soul to death and was numbered with the transgressors; yet he bore the sin of many, and makes intercession for the transgressors." Isaiah 53:10-12 ESV

Through study, we can learn that it was by his blood that his soul was poured out. We all need to understand that his blood was not poured out to be wasted, but to be received.

By taking the cup, we are receiving the lot apportioned to Jesus by the Father, and it is poured from his cup, his vessel, into our lives. The root word for *poterion* is "*pino*" which, figuratively, means to receive into the soul what serves to refresh and strengthen it, nourishing it unto life eternal. There is only one way to receive what is needed to exist as an eternal soul, and that is the soulish nature of Jesus. When we receive him, and drink of his blood, we receive eternal life. This is the only way to the Father, through Christ.

> *"And he took a cup, and when he had given thanks he gave it to them, saying, "Drink of it, all of you, for this is my blood of the covenant, which is poured out for many for the forgiveness of sins. I tell you I will not drink again of this fruit of the vine until that day when I drink it new with you in my Father's kingdom." Matthew 26:27-29 ESV*

I don't want to move on from this topic without highlighting the new blood covenant. This particular type of covenant refers to the last disposition or arrangement one makes of his earthly possessions after his death, a will and testament. For Christ, the blood covenant is his will for us, and in his blood is written the desires of his heart for his possessions. When we receive the blood, we receive the inheritance of the kingdom, that which Christ has asked the Father to give us.

> "When Jesus had spoken these words, he lifted up his eyes to heaven, and said, "Father, the hour has come; glorify your Son that the Son may glorify you, since you have given him authority over all flesh, to give eternal life to all whom you have given him. And this is eternal life, that they know you the only true God, and Jesus Christ whom you have sent. I glorified you on earth, having accomplished the work that you gave me to do. And now, Father, glorify me in your own presence with the glory that I had with you before the world existed. "I have manifested your name to the people whom you gave me out of the world. Yours they were, and you gave them to me, and they have kept your word. Now they know that everything that you have given me is from you. For I have given them the words that you gave me, and they have received them and have come to know in truth that I came from you; and they have believed that you sent me. I am praying for them. I am not praying for the world but for those whom you have given me, for they are yours. All mine are yours, and yours are mine, and I am glorified in them. And I am no longer in the world, but they are in the world, and I am coming to you. Holy Father, keep them in your name, which you have given me, that they may be one, even as we are one. While I was with them, I kept them in your name, which you have given me. I have guarded them, and not one of them has been lost except the son of destruction, that the Scripture might be fulfilled. But now

Chapter 5

I am coming to you, and these things I speak in the world, that they may have my joy fulfilled in themselves. I have given them your word, and the world has hated them because they are not of the world, just as I am not of the world. I do not ask that you take them out of the world, but that you keep them from the evil one. They are not of the world, just as I am not of the world. Sanctify them in the truth; your word is truth. As you sent me into the world, so I have sent them into the world. And for their sake I consecrate myself, that they also may be sanctified in truth. "I do not ask for these only, but also for those who will believe in me through their word, that they may all be one, just as you, Father, are in me, and I in you, that they also may be in us, so that the world may believe that you have sent me. The glory that you have given me I have given to them, that they may be one even as we are one, I in them and you in me, that they may become perfectly one, so that the world may know that you sent me and loved them even as you loved me. Father, I desire that they also, whom you have given me, may be with me where I am, to see my glory that you have given me because you loved me before the foundation of the world. O righteous Father, even though the world does not know you, I know you, and these know that you have sent me. I made known to them your name, and I will continue to make it known, that the love with which you have loved me may be in them, and I in them." John 17:1-26 ESV

6
Imagine for a Moment

When I teach on hearing the voice of the Spirit, or about hearing the thoughts of God, I tend to get asked an interesting question. "How do you know that this isn't just your imagination?"

I find it unfortunate that so many people are afraid of their imaginations in the first place! Is using our imagination a sign of immaturity? Previous to our relationship with Christ, the answer would be yes, but when functioning out of the mind of Christ, I don't believe it is vane to explore with our imaginations. When I hear positive comments regarding the imagination, it is usually from children! Most adults don't like the thought of "entertaining their own minds," unless it is for the sake of sin.

Interestingly enough, when the word is used in Scripture it almost always has a negative connotation to it. Vain imaginations, evil considerations of the heart, and foolish ideas are the types of "imaginations" that we see in the Bible. Yet, we also find exhortations to set our hearts on things to come, or heavenly ideas. The truth about our imagination is that if we use it to stir up natural ideas, we could be reaping the fruit of an unhealthy mentality. Yet, when we explore the realm of the imagination as a result of spiritual influence by the Holy Spirit, we will find ourselves in the midst of an incredible source of revelation!

"If then you have been raised with Christ, seek the things that are above, where Christ is, seated at the right hand of God. Set your minds on things that are above, not on things that are on earth." Colossians 3:1-2 ESV

Exhortations like this are found all throughout Scripture, which is practical enough, being that we serve an unseen God. In order to set our hearts and minds on things which cannot be seen, we will have to use some form of our imaginations. In fact, we are called to live in the realm of faith, which happens to be the opposite of sight. In order to live faithfully, we cannot base our opinions, judgments, or perspectives off of what we see physically.

"He who has prepared us for this very thing is God, who

Chapter 6

has given us the Spirit as a guarantee. So we are always of good courage. We know that while we are at home in the body we are away from the Lord, for we walk by faith, not by sight." 2 Corinthians 5:5-7 ESV

Are our hopes, dreams, desires, aspirations, expectations, and goals not all some form of our imaginations? If we are seeking the Lord on any specific issue, are we not meditating in imaginative thought about his will for those things? Would "considering" not be a form of imagination? Yes, we are full of imaginations, which are not all empty or vain, nor are they all destructive to our relationship with Christ. Furthermore, much of what we hope for in Christ is birthed somewhere in between our hearts and minds, in the place that imaginations are formed.

I love how my children use their imaginations to grow and develop, and I often wish mine had not been suffocated so quickly as I grew older. If were to be honest, we would have to admit that our imaginations are what help us become business owners, inventors, and creators. Even the ways we design and organize our homes and offices come from a place of imagination. First, we internally picture how we might want things to look, and then we apply the work in order to accomplish the goals we formed in our minds. Depending on whether or not our intentional thoughts were formed as a result of natural or spiritual imagination will determine how uniquely inspired the work we accomplish really was by the Holy Spirit.

The ways we write and communicate with others in speech are also formed by what our hearts and minds are set on when we are silent. Therefore, the issue of whether or not our imaginations are healthy for spiritual growth depends on what treasures we have chosen to lay up in our hearts and minds. In order to examine ourselves, we should not only consider what treasures already exist in our hearts, but also what treasures we desire to be placed there.

"Do not lay up for yourselves treasures on earth, where moth and rust destroy and where thieves break in and steal, but lay up for yourselves treasures in heaven, where neither moth nor rust destroys and where thieves do not break in and steal. For where your treasure is, there your heart will be also." Matthew 6:19-21 ESV

"For no good tree bears bad fruit, nor again does a bad tree bear good fruit, for each tree is known by its own fruit. For figs are not gathered from thornbushes, nor are grapes picked from a bramble bush. The good person out of the good treasure of his heart produces good, and the evil person out of his evil treasure produces evil, for out of the abundance of the heart his mouth speaks." Luke 6:43-45 ESV

Christians must watch over what is allowed in and out of our hearts and minds. If Eve had never allowed the lies of the serpent to be at rest within her heart, she would not have considered the result of eating the fruit to be good, pleasing, and desirable. Yet, since she did allow those lies (which were inconsistent with God's spoken word) to make their home within her heart, her decision to eat the fruit was comfortable. Before she ever ate the fruit, she first imagined what it was going to be like to experience the suggested results of Satan's lies. She imagined what it might be like to taste this forbidden fruit, and to be like God, having knowledge of good and evil, and to be nourished from the fruit.

Today, there are too many lies to count being spread throughout the world, not only from Satan, but also through people we meet out in public, or see on tv, radio, social media, or other social platforms. In this generation, we are able to look at the speech and writings of people all over the world in a moment of time. We can watch live-streamed videos from all over the world with the use of the internet. Therefore, we must learn to be careful when listening to any person speak, and be willing to weigh each word in accordance with God's Word, using our spiritual senses of imagination. Depending on what we choose to come into agreement with in our minds, what we allow to take root in our hearts, we too can make comfortable decisions that produce evil and darkness in and around us. For us to identify what lies we may have come into agreement with, and to embrace cleansing from any agreement we have made with words that came to us outside the boundaries of God's Word, we might need to embrace a prayer much like the psalmist entered in Psalm 51.

> *"Behold, you delight in truth in the inward being, and you teach me wisdom in the secret heart. Purge me with hyssop, and I shall be clean; wash me, and I shall be whiter than snow. Let me hear joy and gladness; let the bones that you have broken rejoice. Hide your face from my sins, and blot out all my iniquities. Create in me a clean heart, O God, and renew a right spirit within me. Cast me not away from your presence, and take not your Holy Spirit from me. Restore to me the joy of your salvation, and uphold me with a willing spirit. Then I will teach transgressors your ways, and sinners will return to you." Psalms 51:6-13 ESV*

Our sights should be consistently established on what God values, not on what we value, unless, of course, we are in agreement with God, valuing the same things he does in our hearts and minds. If we can tune our spiritual and mental "dials" in to the streams of knowledge and wisdom flowing from the throne of God in heaven, we can begin to imagine beautiful things that will produce life within us. We can learn to realize and embrace the destinies God has already spoken over our lives without the unnecessary corruption of involving worthless treasures from unhealthy imaginations existing

Chapter 6

within our hearts.

Not only that, but when we partner with heaven in our desires, dreams, and goals, the enemy cannot destroy them, for the treasures of the kingdom that we hope to release on the earth in the fulfilment of those things are kept up in heaven. If we trust God, banking on him, we can rest assured that everything we need to fulfill our tasks can be quickly withdrawn in due season from the treasures of heaven that we have built up with him in the secret place.

"On the last day of the feast, the great day, Jesus stood up and cried out, "If anyone thirsts, let him come to me and drink. Whoever believes in me, as the Scripture has said, 'Out of his heart will flow rivers of living water.'" Now this he said about the Spirit, whom those who believed in him were to receive, for as yet the Spirit had not been given, because Jesus was not yet glorified." John 7:37-39 ESV

7
Living from the Kingdom

"Jesus said to her, "Woman, believe me, the hour is coming when neither on this mountain nor in Jerusalem will you worship the Father. You worship what you do not know; we worship what we know, for salvation is from the Jews. But the hour is coming, and is now here, when the true worshipers will worship the Father in spirit and truth, for the Father is seeking such people to worship him. God is spirit, and those who worship him must worship in spirit and truth." John 4:21-24 ESV

"In him we have obtained an inheritance, having been predestined according to the purpose of him who works all things according to the counsel of his will, so that we who were the first to hope in Christ might be to the praise of his glory. In him

you also, when you heard the word of truth, the gospel of your salvation, and believed in him, were sealed with the promised Holy Spirit, who is the guarantee of our inheritance until we acquire possession of it, to the praise of his glory. For this reason, because I have heard of your faith in the Lord Jesus and your love toward all the saints, I do not cease to give thanks for you, remembering you in my prayers, that the God of our Lord Jesus Christ, the Father of glory, may give you the Spirit of wisdom and of revelation in the knowledge of him, having the eyes of your hearts enlightened, that you may know what is the hope to which he has called you, what are the riches of his glorious inheritance in the saints, and what is the immeasurable greatness of his power toward us who believe, according to the working of his great might that he worked in Christ when he raised him from the dead and seated him at his right hand in the heavenly places, far above all rule and authority and power and dominion, and above every name that is named, not only in this age but also in the one to come. And he put all things under his feet and gave him as head over all things to the church, which is his body, the fullness of him who fills all in all." Ephesians 1:11-23 ESV

What does it mean to live from the kingdom? What does it mean to worship in spirit and truth? The focus of this chapter will remain on these aspects of Christian life. My aim is to highlight the importance of living from a mature kingdom perspective while we carry out the continuing work of Christ on the earth. To begin, I want to take us on a journey through some dynamic aspects of spiritual truth, and the power of a truthful spirit.

The word, "truth" can be interpreted in many ways. After defining some of the most important truths, we will go over a few aspects of the applications of them. This will help to broaden our understanding of the importance of keeping and bearing with the truth itself.

There are two main revelations of truth that reveal God's provisions and promises that have been made available to us:

The Word of God,

The Son of God.

By seeking to understand more about God's Word, we can learn to live in accordance with it. By coming to know Jesus more, we can learn to come into submission to him in all areas of life, through love.

The Word of God

The written and recorded Word of God, both Old and New Testament, is made up of perfect theology. It is the perfect pathway for acquiring doctrine, revelation, and tools for application in our lives. Without the written Word of God, we would be completely lost. However, because the Bible has been compiled and presented to us in perfect form, we are able to learn and apply all of the principles and commands found in it.

> *"But as for you, continue in what you have learned and have firmly believed, knowing from whom you learned it and how from childhood you have been acquainted with the sacred writings, which are able to make you wise for salvation through faith in Christ Jesus. All Scripture is breathed out by God and profitable for teaching, for reproof, for correction, and for training in righteousness, that the man of God may be complete, equipped for every good work." 2 Timothy 3:14-17 ESV*

It is important to understand that although the Bible contains the truth, the work has not yet been completed. It has been given to us by God so that we can learn to reflect its make-up and become equipped for every good work. We cannot live under the suggestion that all of the work has been finished, or that all of the world has already been saved through Christ. Unless we express the person of Jesus through our own lives, as a result of the edification that comes to us from the Word in us, the world may never come to know this Jesus who we claim to know and love.

Because of our love for God and his Word, we are able to represent Christ to the world that does not know him. As we continually encounter Jesus through the Word, we will be made able to reflect his image and bear his name. Although our personal relationships with God should dictate how we are led, the Word of God is the truth that supplies us with the wisdom and knowledge needed to appropriate what we seek to accomplish in and through him.

Where we read, what we study, and how we learn from the Bible should always be in tune with the spiritual convictions we receive by the Spirit of God in our hearts. When we live from that place of communion with God, the Word becomes a living, breathing, active force which empowers us to prevail in any task. Therefore, I encourage the church to be full of the wisdom and knowledge we find in Scripture. We ought never to neglect study, but instead embrace it to show ourselves approved. As the Word is received, we will be able to show forth its virtue in daily life.

> *"You yourselves are our letter of recommendation, written on our hearts, to be known and read by all. And you show that you are a letter from Christ delivered by us, written not with ink but with the Spirit of the living God, not on tablets of stone but on tablets of human hearts. Such is the confidence that we have through Christ toward God. Not that we are sufficient in ourselves to claim anything as coming from us, but our sufficiency is from God, who has made us sufficient to be ministers of a new covenant, not of the letter but of the Spirit. For the letter kills, but the Spirit gives life." 2 Corinthians 3:2-6 ESV*

The Word of God is a precious gift given to us so that all who call upon his name might be able to learn from him while remaining in the body of flesh. For this reason, we can learn to utilize what we find in Scripture to align ourselves with God who is spirit, even though we are still living in the flesh. God has given us the Holy Spirit in order that our spirits might be able to align with his will. He has given his own Son's blood on the altar to make atonement for our souls, allowing us to receive the soulish nature of Christ himself through receiving the mind of Christ, so that our minds can come into agreement with his will. He has given us the Word in the form of written text so that our bodies of flesh can come into agreement with his will through the physical senses of sight, touch, and sound.

To understand how to apply the Word of God in our daily lives, I want to focus on the findings in a set of scriptures that reveals what the Word of God does for us.

The Word Gives Life

"But he answered, "It is written, "'Man shall not live by bread alone, but by every word that comes from the mouth of God.'" Matthew 4:4 ESV

God's Word not only supplies us with knowledge, but it also supplies us with life. This verse speaks of God's spoken Word, which was received by all those who wrote Scripture. Because all Scripture is God-breathed, we know that all Scripture came from the mouth of God – his voice. In the same way, we too can be restored in the life of our flesh by seeking God while he may be found, and being taught from his lips. We are not only nourished by the spoken Word, but also by the written Word, which was God-breathed before it was written. This seems impossible, but those who have spent extended periods of time in fasting will know this to be true. When I have fasted in the past, God has nourished my flesh body by his spoken and written word, causing hunger to leave me and for my body to be fully nourished in every way!

The Word of God Offers Blessings

"But he said, "Blessed rather are those who hear the word of God and keep it!" Luke 11:28 ESV

The word used in this scripture for "blessed" actually means to be happy. Happiness is circumstantial rather than ongoing. Therefore, the blessing that comes from hearing the Word of God is conditional to actually hearing it, whether by someone reading aloud the words of the Bible, the preaching of the Word, or by the voice of the Holy Spirit. Whichever way the word of God is heard, if it is kept, a blessing of happiness will come.

The word "keep" here actually means to guard, protect, and observe. Whenever one hears the Word of God and guards it, keeping tabs on its message and the fruit of it, he will be blessed in overwhelming happiness. Happiness is achievable for anyone who watches over the Word with care.

The Word Produces Faith

"So faith comes by hearing, and hearing by the word of Christ." Romans 10:17 ESV

Those who have already come to know Jesus do not necessarily have perfect faith. The Word teaches that Christ is the Author and Perfecter of our faith. Our faith has an Author! He has written faith down in the words of the Bible, and also speaks them to his church. Whenever any of us are lacking in faith, we should get into the Word. Reading the Bible and listening to the voice of the Shepherd are the primary routes to receiving new levels of faith in our lives.

There are times when we are believing God for the healing of a sick family member or friend. In those times, it's not always easy to have faith. We may have a desire for these people to be healed, but do we have faith that they will be? We may know that God can heal them, but do we know that he will? There will be times all throughout our lives when we need more faith, specific faith. In those times,

Chapter 7

we can find faith by hearing the Word of God.

The Word Provides Power

"For the word of the cross is folly to those who are perishing, but to us who are being saved it is the power of God." 1 Corinthians 1:18 ESV

Like faith, power does not come in a full package. There will be times in our lives that require higher levels of power. Power, in this form, describes strength and ability. The power that is received through the Word of Christ, the Gospel, is the power to save. Because Christ has accomplished on earth what no man could accomplish, all those who call upon his name shall be saved. To be saved by Christ is to be healed physically, spiritually, and mentally, saved from sin and death, and delivered from the molestations of the enemy. For those who do not believe in Jesus, the Gospel does not produce power, but for those who believe on the Son of God who came to set them free, it is the power of God for current and future salvation. Jesus is the only provider of this type of power, and God has made a way for us to receive his power by grace through faith. For it is by grace that we have been saved, through faith, and that occurs when we call on his name. The Word of God is the written word that speaks clearly to us regarding the identity of Jesus.

The Word is Active

"For the word of God is living and active, sharper than any two-edged sword, piercing to the division of soul and of spirit, of joints and of marrow, and discerning the thoughts and intentions of the heart." Hebrews 4:12 ESV

One of the most interesting verses in the Bible, in my opinion, is Hebrews 4:12. This verse speaks of a living Word, one which is able to separate all aspects of life in order to establish purpose in the hearts, minds, and bodies of those who call on the name of Jesus. The division of soul and spirit refers to the help we receive through the Word in identifying all sources of spiritual influences which are bent on affecting the way we think. When the spirit and soul have been separated, we can learn to understand what has been deposited into our minds, and whether or not what we think is lined up with the Word of God.

The division of joints and marrow speaks specifically to the workings of our souls. Leviticus 17 teaches us that the soul is in the blood and that the blood is the soul. A study of the physical body can teach us that the blood is formed in the marrow of the bones, which are connected by joints that allow limited movement. When the Word of God "pierces to the division of joints and marrow," it divides that which guards our former soulish nature from the movement and influence of the powerful blood of Jesus that is now at work in our lives. The division of joints and marrow answers the question, "What does God say that the blood of Jesus does for me?"

The "discerning of the thoughts and intentions of the heart" speaks to those aspects of our conscious and intuitive thoughts, which may or may not have been affected by the working of demons, angels, or the Holy Spirit. Regardless of how those thoughts and intentions have been developed, the Word of God is constant in its power to expose what does not line up with the knowledge of God. If we allow the Word to work in our lives (to convict us of unhealthy thoughts and intentions in our hearts), God will rightly manage not only what goes into our hearts and minds, but also what manifests itself out of our bodies through speech and actions. What a privilege it is to have access to both the spoken and written Word of God!

The Son of God

The Word of God is one vehicle that God has chosen to deliver truth to the world. The most important truth in the written Word of God is the revelation of the roles of Jesus. It gives us incredible detail throughout both the Old and New Testaments of the character, personality, and love of Jesus the Messiah, the Son, the Lord, and the King.

Each position that Jesus holds in Scripture should also be held in our hearts when we consider who he is to each of us, individually. These perspectives of "knowing Jesus" open realms of encounter for us that are purposed to help us learn how to prevail over the present darkness we face on earth, through him. There are various seasons of warfare that will be faced by us throughout our lives, regardless of interests we might have in enduring them. In fact, spiritual warfare will increase as we await his second coming. As this takes place, we will need to know Jesus more. To know Jesus, is to know victory. The Word reveals to us four major perspectives of his identity that will help us unfold the mysteries of these "realms of knowing Jesus."

> *"Jesus said to him, "I am the way, and the truth, and the life. No one comes to the Father except through me." John 14:6 ESV*

As we draw near to the second coming of Christ, we should press on toward the identity of the overcomers. To become overcomers, we need to recognize our relationship with Jesus in four major positions. Without honoring him in these roles in our lives, we cannot come into submission under his Lordship in those areas. Without being subject to the Lordship of Jesus in every aspect, we remain vulnerable to defeat in the last days. To make this simple, let's make sure that we understand his identity as the first true overcomer. He overcame all of the obstacles set before him by man and the powers of darkness, and he never sinned. When we come to know him personally, in respect to these four positions, he is able to reveal himself through us because of our awareness and knowledge of his true character.

Relying on mere theology alone will never work as a means to salvation. Knowing Jesus personally, however, develops the spirit of the overcomer in ways that we might never perceive possible. To be blunt, nearly controversial, I could suggest that we must not "accept" Jesus, but rather we must know him. The Word of God never teaches us to accept Jesus! It does teach us to accept his Gospel, but our relationship with Christ is to be more than a relationship with a doctrine, it is to be a relationship with our Lord.

If anyone seeks to enter the kingdom of God, he must first believe on Jesus, receiving him personally. Of course, the Gospel of Christ is the vehicle that delivers the faith-based reality of the person of Jesus to an unbeliever. Because of this, we must accept the Gospel of Christ separate from believing in the person of Christ. Without distinguishing between the two, many who think they know Jesus, have really only accepted a teaching in logical reasoning, but have never actually met the Lord personally. Those who have never met the Lord personally will not know his voice, and cannot be led by him. Instead, they will follow the idea of a teaching, but never experience personal servanthood or friendship with the Lord.

The four positions that we need to recognize in the Son of God are as follows:

Jesus as Messiah,

Jesus as the quickening spirit (anointing),

Jesus as King,

Jesus as Lord.

8
Jesus as Messiah

Throughout the Old Testament there were many prophetic utterances that pointed to the reality of a Messiah. These prophecies were fulfilled by Jesus in accordance with the words given. We know this by the personal testimony of Jesus himself, before and after his sacrifice on the cross and his resurrection from the grave.

> "Then he said to them, "These are my words that I spoke to you while I was still with you, that everything written about me in the Law of Moses and the Prophets and the Psalms must be fulfilled." Then he opened their minds to understand the Scriptures, and said to them, "Thus it is written, that the Christ should suffer and on the third day rise from the dead, and that repentance and forgiveness of sins should be proclaimed in his name to all

nations, beginning from Jerusalem. You are witnesses of these things. And behold, I am sending the promise of my Father upon you. But stay in the city until you are clothed with power from on high." Luke 24:44-49 ESV

"That very day two of them were going to a village named Emmaus, about seven miles from Jerusalem, and they were talking with each other about all these things that had happened. While they were talking and discussing together, Jesus himself drew near and went with them. But their eyes were kept from recognizing him. And he said to them, "What is this conversation that you are holding with each other as you walk?" And they stood still, looking sad. Then one of them, named Cleopas, answered him, "Are you the only visitor to Jerusalem who does not know the things that have happened there in these days?" And he said to them, "What things?" And they said to him, "Concerning Jesus of Nazareth, a man who was a prophet mighty in deed and word before God and all the people, and how our chief priests and rulers delivered him up to be condemned to death, and crucified him. But we had hoped that he was the one to redeem Israel. Yes, and besides all this, it is now the third day since these things happened. Moreover, some women of our company amazed us. They were at the tomb early in the morning, and when they did not find his body, they came back saying that they had even seen a vision of angels, who said that he was alive. Some of those who were with us went to the tomb and found it just as the women had said, but him they did not see." And he said to them, "O

Chapter 8

foolish ones, and slow of heart to believe all that the prophets have spoken! Was it not necessary that the Christ should suffer these things and enter into his glory?" And beginning with Moses and all the Prophets, he interpreted to them in all the Scriptures the things concerning himself." Luke 24:13-27 ESV

Accepting the testimony of the Word, specifically the Gospel of Christ, literally means receiving in our hearts that the Lord Jesus fulfilled the Messianic prophecies of the Old Testament. Accepting it as truth even though we didn't see those fulfillments take place in person is truly what it means to believe the Gospel. When we accept those truths found in Scripture, we become ready to personally meet our Messiah. The word "Messiah" in both Hebrew and Greek means "anointed one," which is also the same definition for the word "Christ." When we identify him as "Jesus Christ," we must realize that Christ is not necessarily a part of his name, but rather, it is the position he holds in the world and in the church. The name, "Jesus Christ" actually describes Jesus as the anointed one of God who was spoken of and prophesied about in the Old Testament! As elementary as that seems, some do not understand that what we are really saying is "Jesus the Anointed" or "Jesus the Messiah."

One of the most famous (if not the most famous) verses of the Bible is John 3:16.

> "For God so loved the world, that he gave his only Son, that whoever believes in him should not perish but have eternal life." John 3:16 ESV

Out of context, many have suggested and even taught that the fulfillment of Messianic prophecies by Jesus was finished in order to save the whole world. Of course, the verse is most always quoted out of context, which is why many have believed it to be a universal scripture for all mankind. If we continue reading this passage, the truth of his Messianic fulfillment becomes a gateway to salvation only for those who are willing to believe in him personally.

> "For God so loved the world, that he gave his only Son, that whoever believes in him should not perish but have eternal life. For God did not send his Son into the world to condemn the world, but in order that the world might be saved through him. Whoever believes in him is not condemned, but whoever does not believe is condemned already, because he has not believed in the name of the only Son of God. And this is the judgment: the light has come into the world, and people loved the darkness rather than the light because their works were evil. For everyone who does wicked things hates the light and does not come to the light, lest his works should be exposed. But whoever does what is true comes to the light, so that it may be clearly seen that his works have been carried out in God." John 3:16-21 ESV

In this passage, the word "world" is describing who and what

Jesus came to save. In Greek, it is "*kosmos*," which describes the universe in its entirety. Specific to this verse, it refers to the ungodly multitude of men who have, through sin, become alienated from God. The fallen nature of man, which all are born into, is not spiritual, but is carnal, and therefore is hostile to the cause of Christ. The purpose for the events carried out in the fulfillment of the Gospel each happened in order to realign the spirituality of men with the grace intended to be given them by God. The Gospel, itself, is spiritual good news. Therefore, it is not to be received by carnal minds, but instead is to be accepted by spiritual minds in order to activate the grace provided through Christ's role in fulfilling it.

With this in mind, we must understand that the reality of eternal punishment for sinners still exists. For those men and women who refuse to receive this Gospel for themselves, and who neglect the eternal need to believe in Jesus, their eternal punishment will be in hell. For those of us who by accepting the Gospel as a provision of spiritual purity profess our reception of the Gospel message, although we were previously sinners, eternal punishment is deferred by God in the power of grace through faith. This, of course is not a work of our own, but is a scandalous outpouring of love that we can all receive because of the provisions made through Christ for eternal salvation from hell.

To appreciate our need to know Jesus as the Messiah, we need to understand some sound theological principles. Notice that in the above verses, salvation had become available to the entire world through Christ, the Son of God. It states that whoever does not believe in him as the Messiah is already condemned, but those who believe would have eternal life. What this means, is that God has chosen to leave the option of salvation up to the sinner. The principles we need to understand about God's ruling are those of predestination, predetermination, and free will.

There are things that God has sovereignly chosen to provide for us in particular times and seasons of our lives, such as the Law, the Gospel, salvation, the dispensation of grace, and many other examples. These provisions are those that make up the "predetermined will of God." These are those opportunities that have been laid out for us by God through thousands of years of ministry, in order to that we might learn to set our minds to receive the provisions made available to us by God. As long as we meet the conditions he has provided in great detail, we will receive the provisions that come with them.

There are also some things that have been predestined by God to occur such as the initial creation, each of our conceptions in the womb, the good works that are to be carried out in the fulfilling of the Great Commission, and the second coming of Christ. These predestined events could not have, and cannot be, overridden, revoked, or controlled by man. Although each person is individually responsible for how he or she reacts to these predestined events, we are not able to dissuade the Lord God from doing what he has already chosen to do!

For example, in John 3 we see that salvation has been made available to the entire world. For this to happen, God predestined that man would be created, predetermined that they would have access to a relationship with him, and allowed them to be able to make the choice to decide whether or not they would be obedient to those provisions. As we understand it, Adam and Eve failed to meet God's conditions in the Garden of Eden, and the provisions of eternal life were stripped from them as a result of their failure. God, therefore, predestined that there would be a law set in place to expose sin and a Gospel carried out by his own Son to fulfill the law, allowing for the predetermination that salvation would be made available through his Son in the dispensation of grace for a time.

These words I've begun using have been thrown around church doctrine for years in many different ways. Predestination is a major topic in biblical theology, and one which many disagree upon. Because there are so many different doctrines, I sense the need to continually clarify my personal understanding of these words.

Predestination describes either events in time, or provisions and realities, which God has predestined to occur in their proper times and seasons. These things, again, cannot be changed or altered to meet our needs because they have been predestined from before the creation of the world. None of us made the decision to be born into the world. Our parents may feel that they had a part to play in the process, and indeed they did, yet it was God who predestined man to be able to procreate, and it is God who chooses whether or not we are born male or female. These things cannot be chosen, changed, or manipulated by soulish thought or desires, even though many people today, unfortunately, believe that it is possible to choose gender after birth.

Predetermination is a word that describes God's decisions to make provisions available to man in various times and seasons, but these provisions are those that can be altered by man in accordance with our obedience to the conditions he chooses to lay before us. For example, salvation was predetermined by God to be made available to man, through Christ, and the provision has been made for us to enter into that salvation. However, each individual man or woman is given the power of choosing whether or not they will meet the conditions of receiving salvation. We know that these conditions include believing in Jesus, knowing him and receiving him personally as Messiah, and being born again. Unless the conditions of faith are met by choice, salvation is not received by any man. Although God predetermined by his own will that none should perish, it is up to each man individually to choose whether or not he will believe in Christ. Even still, we must understand that because God first chose us to be adopted into the family of God, his own provision of unconditional love is what empowers us to be able to apply faith and receive salvation. We have been predestined to be given faith, and predetermined to enter into salvation under the condition that we take hold of the faith already provided to us through Christ.

The two major aspects of God's predestined and predetermined provisions are those of signs and conditions. By learning what roles these signs and conditions play, we can more easily step into a matured understanding of God's will in our personal lives, our families, spiritual family, and even the cities, states, and nations in which we live.

Whatever God has predestined to occur will always be accompanied by signs. Whenever God predetermines anything he always provides conditions that must be met.

When the Son of God, Jesus, was born into the world, the signs of a virgin birth and a bright star in the sky accompanied his entrance. When the gospel of the kingdom came forth into the world, signs accompanied the message then, and still do today. When future predestined events occur, signs will accompany them. For example, Jesus spoke of specific signs that will point to the end of days and his second coming. These specific signs will cause us to be aware that our redemption draws near. When the antichrist who has been predestined to come on the scene arrives, there will be signs accompanying him, such as the abomination of desolation or the mark of the beast, or even a wound to the head that is miraculously healed. These are all examples of scenarios where signs accompanied, or will accompany, the predestined will of God.

When predetermined provisions of salvation, healing, and deliverance are available, we can receive them as we meet the conditions. If we choose to receive salvation through faith in Christ Jesus, we must meet the conditions of faith. If we need to receive healing, we must meet the condition of believing that by his stripes we have been healed already. As Christians, if we need deliverance from the molestations of the enemy after having received salvation, we must meet the conditions of repentance and renunciation of sins, transgressions, iniquities, and covenants made with the demonic in order to receive deliverance.

One provision not understood by all is the grace that is administered through the gifts of the Holy Spirit. This provision helps us to carry out the Great Commission in power and love. For us to step into these provisions of grace, we must obey the commands given to us by Jesus to love the Lord our God with all our heart, all our mind, all our soul, and all our strength, and to love our neighbors as ourselves. If we meet these conditions, we will be made able to carry out the Great Commission of discipling nations in the name of Jesus. When those conditions are met, not in order to be saved, but in order to remain in Christ and be sacrificially obedient, we will be empowered by grace to function in the gifts of the Holy Spirit in constant, tangible ways. These gifts include those of teaching, leadership, mercy, exhortation, faith, healing, and others found in Romans 12, 1 Corinthians 12 & 14, and Ephesians 4.

Because God wanted to make these predetermined provisions available to us so that we would be able to experience his power and love on the earth, he predestined the times and seasons in which man would be given access to these provisions. God gave the Law at a specific time to Moses as a provision for righteousness, including the prophetic acts of atonement for cleansing in the place of unfulfilled law, knowing that man would be unable to completely fulfill that law outside of the work of his Son, the Messiah and Savior of the world.

He predestined the time of his Son's birth into the world in a body of flesh, and the work he performed during his earthly ministry. He predestined the sufferings which Jesus had to undergo, and even the resurrection from the grave as another prophetic act of the glory he will one day reveal in his people. Because the Son of God has come in the flesh to fulfill the law, and because of his finishing work of atonement on the cross, all who make the decision to believe in him have access to the provisions of grace God has already predetermined to reveal through his Son, including resurrection!

Although God has predestined when that time will come to a close, and although he has predetermined a period of grace and a salvation through his Son, he does not take full control of the world in order to fulfill his own desires. God's will is that none should perish, but that all would believe on his Son and receive eternal life. He has made this entirely possible by offering his own Son on the cross for the sins of the world! However, before we can enter the kingdom, and before we can inherit salvation, conditions must be met. Just as God gave Adam and Eve conditions in the Garden of Eden, we too have been given conditions on the earth. If we never believe in Christ, and come to know him as our personal Messiah, accepting the reality that his Gospel work was carried out for each of us individually, we will not enter the kingdom. Although God desires that none should perish, he leaves the choice of receiving salvation up to us.

Chapter 8

If we choose to accept the Gospel and believe in Jesus as the Son of God, the Messiah and Savior of the world, we receive ongoing and eternal salvation. If we choose to reject this message, we will be forced to endure eternal fire and separation from God in hell. For those who do believe in Christ and follow his commands to love God and people, there are wondrous works for us to walk in, times and seasons of provision by which we can minister effectively in the Great Commission. My prayer is that all who come to know Jesus as their personal Messiah would become familiar with the Word of God so that we can effectively minister to the world by meeting the conditions of God's predetermined will, and know the signs of the times in God's predestined will. By choice, and in love, we as believers must choose to enter into the perfect provisions that God has made available to us through the Messiah, Jesus!

9
The Quickening Spirit

Knowing Jesus as our personal Messiah is the key to receiving salvation through Christ, by faith. Knowing Jesus as the quickening spirit is crucial to walking in the power of his anointing while we carry out the great commission. We will never be able to effectively reach people in the ministry of reconciliation unless we encounter the quickening spirit of Christ and come to know him in power. Jesus did not minister on his own accord, but only did what he saw his Father doing. He only said what he heard his Father saying, and that was possible because he had been anointed by the Holy Spirit to do good works.

To understand the anointing of Christ, which is available to every believer, we need to understand what it consists of, and why he was anointed in the first place. The anointing, or quickening spirit, of Christ, is the spiritual make-up that empowered him to overcome the enemy and the world in the flesh. In my first book, "Prevailing Soul," I wrote about how the quickening spirit is the same spirit that kept Jesus from speaking out while enduring the cross and the moments leading up to it. It is the spirit that caused the disciples to worship the Lord in the middle of a prison cell with shackles on their ankles! We need to be quickened by the quickening spirit of the Lord even today as we endure through trials!

We see the seven aspects of this anointing clearly in Isaiah 11.

"There shall come forth a shoot from the stump of Jesse, and a branch from his roots shall bear fruit. And the Spirit of the Lord shall rest upon him, the Spirit of wisdom and understanding, the Spirit of counsel and might, the Spirit of knowledge and the fear of the Lord. And his delight shall be in the fear of the Lord. He shall not judge by what his eyes see, or decide disputes by what his ears hear, but with righteousness he shall judge the poor, and decide with equity for the meek of the earth; and he shall strike the earth with the rod of his mouth, and with the breath of his lips he shall kill the wicked. Righteousness shall be the belt of his waist, and faithfulness the belt of his loins." Isaiah 11:1-5 ESV

These verses describe to us the ways in which he was anointed in his spirit to do good works. In the Gospel of Luke, Jesus quotes Isaiah and proclaims these works as his own personal mission!

"And he came to Nazareth, where he had been brought up. And as was his custom, he went to the synagogue on the Sabbath day, and he stood up to read. And the scroll of the prophet Isaiah was given to him. He unrolled the scroll and found the place where it was written,

"The Spirit of the Lord is upon me, because he has anointed me to proclaim good news to the poor. He has sent me to proclaim liberty to the captives and recovering of sight to the blind, to set at liberty those who are oppressed, to proclaim the year of the Lord's favor."

And he rolled up the scroll and gave it back to the attendant and sat down. And the eyes of all in the synagogue were fixed on him. And he began to say to them, "Today this Scripture has been fulfilled in your hearing." Luke 4:16-21 ESV

Today, we can walk in this same spiritual anointing, carrying with us the same authority and power that he carried because he has given us his own spirit for that very purpose! In fact, right before Jesus breathed his last breath on the cross, he said "Father, into your hands I commit my spirit." Later, 1 Corinthians 15:45 tells us that Christ himself became a life-giving spirit! We know through our previous studies in this book that spirits are made to dwell inside the bodies of humans. Whether they are demon spirits, human spirits, or the Holy Spirit, they can all find rest within human bodies. The word tells us in John 14:23,

"Jesus answered him, "If anyone loves me, he will keep my word, and my Father will love him, and we will come to him and make our home with him." John 14:23 ESV

How is it that they will come to us and make their home with us? It is by the quickening spirit of Christ!

"Thus it is written, "The first man Adam became a living being"; the last Adam became a life-giving spirit." 1 Corinthians 15:45

Jesus became a "life-giving" or "quickening" spirit so that we might receive life from him now, not requiring that we wait until his return to quicken us fully into eternal life in our resurrection nature. The life that is received from him is not our own, but is his! This is why we can know with assurance that we have been made alive with Christ! Not only are we provided eternal life with him through salvation, but we are also endued with his spiritual resurrection life while we remain on the earth so that we might be able to minister in his same anointing until he returns.

For us to maturely comprehend how the spiritual attributes of Jesus are able to anoint us through the Holy Spirit, we must consider an important aspect of the Holy Trinity. Jesus taught us that he himself was in the Father, and that the Father was in him. This tells us that, although separate from each other, the two somehow dwell together as one. The same perspective is accurate when thinking of the Holy Spirit. When we abide in Christ, the Father makes his home in us separate from the indwelling of the Holy Spirit. Also, the Son is in us and we in him as long as we remain in him. Therefore, through the Spirit, the spiritual attributes of the Father, Son, and Holy Spirit can manifest in us on the earth.

God the Father manifests through the spiritual gifts mentioned in Romans 12, the Holy Spirit manifests through us by the gifts mentioned in 1 Corinthians 12, and Jesus manifests through us by the service or "ministry" gifts mentioned in Ephesians 4. God has predestined us for good works, and predetermined which gifts would work in each of our lives at any given time. As we submit to his lead in the Spirit, by abiding in Christ and seeking first the kingdom, these gifts manifest in us and through us by his Spirit, and in accordance with his will.

In fact, by receiving the baptism of the Holy Spirit and being endued with power from on high, we are made able to know in part and prophesy in part in relation to God's predestined and predetermined times and seasons. Among other gifts that we can walk in during our lives as believers, prophecy is one of the most influential.

We see various types of revelations received in the Old Testament by Prophets who had visitations from the Holy Spirit. During these visitations, something spiritual occurred in their lives. Often, we see it represented with these words, "The hand of the Lord came upon him," or "The Spirit of the Lord came upon him." Whenever this would happen, these saints of old would begin to manifest the presence and the nature of God in their actions, speech, and leadership. They were made able to speak out regarding God's times, seasons, and predetermined judgments as well as the provisions of conditions which would keep people safe from those judgments. This is similar to the work of the quickening spirit, and is a perfect visual representation of what happens to us even today when we are quickened by him.

The reason why this is so important is that, without the recognition of when we are being quickened by the Lord, we may not understand the reason or purpose for why we do what we do. The more sensitive we become to the presence of the Lord, the better we will become at recognizing when he is strengthening us in spirit for a specific reason. For instance, Revelation 19:10 tells us that the testimony of Jesus is the spirit of prophecy. When the spirit of prophecy stirs up within us, prompting us to speak out things we know not of, hidden truths revealed to us by God in season, it is not we who speak, but Christ who speaks through us! When sudden bursts of prophetic thoughts enter our minds and cause our hearts to beat faster, we're not just experiencing some random emotion, we are probably being quickened in spirit to prophesy!

Examples of these provisions of conditions are seen in the relationships between God and men like Abraham and Jonah. God agreed with Abraham that if there were even ten righteous people in Sodom and Gomorrah, he would not destroy it. Of course, we know that there were not even ten, and they were destroyed. They were destroyed because they did not meet the conditions agreed to by God.

"So the men turned from there and went toward Sodom, but Abraham still stood before the Lord. Then Abraham drew near and said, "Will you indeed sweep away the righteous with the wicked? Suppose there are fifty righteous within the city. Will you then sweep away the place and not spare it for the fifty righteous who are in it? Far be it from you to do such a thing, to put the righteous to death with the wicked, so that the righteous fare as the wicked! Far be that from you! Shall not the Judge of all the earth do what is just?" And the Lord said, "If I find at Sodom fifty righteous in the city, I will spare the whole place for their sake."

Abraham answered and said, "Behold, I have undertaken to speak to the Lord, I who am but dust and ashes. Suppose five of the fifty righteous are lacking. Will you destroy the whole city for lack of five?" And he said, "I will not destroy it if I find forty-five there." Again he spoke to him and said, "Suppose forty are found there." He answered, "For the sake of forty I will not do it." Then he said, "Oh let not the Lord be angry, and I will speak. Suppose thirty are found there." He answered, "I will not do it, if I find thirty there." He said, "Behold, I have undertaken to speak to the Lord. Suppose twenty are found there." He answered, "For the sake of twenty I will not destroy it." Then he said, "Oh let not the Lord be angry, and I will speak again but this once. Suppose ten are found there." He answered, "For the sake of ten I will not destroy it." And the Lord went his way, when he had finished speaking to Abraham, and Abraham returned to his place." Genesis 18:22-33 ESV

"The sun had risen on the earth when Lot came to Zoar. Then the Lord rained on Sodom and Gomorrah sulfur and fire from the Lord out of heaven. And he overthrew those cities, and all the valley, and all the inhabitants of the cities, and what grew on the ground." Genesis 19:23-25 ESV

Jonah delivered a prophetic word to the people of Nineveh. Because they had received this word, they knew that God had given them an opportunity to repent. The people believed God that destruction was coming to their kingdom, and that it would surely be overthrown in forty days just as the prophet had spoken. Because they accepted this word, and began to repent and fast, turning from

Chapter 9

their wicked ways, God spared them! The wisdom of the king of Nineveh was apparent in this situation as he sent out a proclamation. The word of the Lord here was their provision of condition, and even though the Lord never spoke through Jonah of a time of repentance, they did so in wisdom. God spared them because of this reaction to the word! This is another great example of a revelation of God's predetermined time and season of destruction, delivered in the word of a specific time period of forty days.

> *"Then the word of the Lord came to Jonah the second time, saying, "Arise, go to Nineveh, that great city, and call out against it the message that I tell you." So Jonah arose and went to Nineveh, according to the word of the Lord. Now Nineveh was an exceedingly great city, three days' journey in breadth. Jonah began to go into the city, going a day's journey. And he called out, "Yet forty days, and Nineveh shall be overthrown!" And the people of Nineveh believed God. They called for a fast and put on sackcloth, from the greatest of them to the least of them.*
>
> *The word reached the king of Nineveh, and he arose from his throne, removed his robe, covered himself with sackcloth, and sat in ashes. And he issued a proclamation and published through Nineveh, "By the decree of the king and his nobles: Let neither man nor beast, herd nor flock, taste anything. Let them not feed or drink water, but let man and beast be covered with sackcloth, and let them call out mightily to God. Let everyone turn from his evil way and from the violence that is in his hands. Who knows?*

God may turn and relent and turn from his fierce anger, so that we may not perish."

When God saw what they did, how they turned from their evil way, God relented of the disaster that he had said he would do to them, and he did not do it." Jonah 3:1-10 ESV

We also see New Testament prophetic words that reveal God's predetermined and predestined will in the realm of times and season, even with the provisions of conditions that can be met. In fact, there are some of these conditions that God revealed through prophetic words that come with rewards, such as the rewards or the overcomers in the seven church ages. These are prophetic utterances that not only prophesy of church cultures, but also their specific corrections. It would only be wise of us to respond to these rebukes and conditions with maturity and respect, regardless of the theological understandings of when these times actually come to pass. Whether some aspects of them have already passed, are in affect presently, or even if they are to come, we must be willing to receive conviction from the Holy Spirit in these areas, and respond in humility in order to receive the fullness of the provisions revealed.

"To the angel of the church in Ephesus write: 'The words of him who holds the seven stars in his right hand, who walks among the seven golden lampstands.

Chapter 9

"'I know your works, your toil and your patient endurance, and how you cannot bear with those who are evil, but have tested those who call themselves apostles and are not, and found them to be false. I know you are enduring patiently and bearing up for my name's sake, and you have not grown weary. But I have this against you, that you have abandoned the love you had at first. Remember therefore from where you have fallen; repent, and do the works you did at first. If not, I will come to you and remove your lampstand from its place, unless you repent. Yet this you have: you hate the works of the Nicolaitans, which I also hate. He who has an ear, let him hear what the Spirit says to the churches. To the one who conquers I will grant to eat of the tree of life, which is in the paradise of God.'

To the Church in Smyrna

"And to the angel of the church in Smyrna write: 'The words of the first and the last, who died and came to life.

"'I know your tribulation and your poverty (but you are rich) and the slander of those who say that they are Jews and are not, but are a synagogue of Satan. Do not fear what you are about to suffer. Behold, the devil is about to throw some of you into prison, that you may be tested, and for ten days you will have tribulation. Be faithful unto death, and I will give you the crown of life. He who has an ear, let him hear what the Spirit says to the churches. The one who conquers will not be hurt by the second death.'

To the Church in Pergamum

"And to the angel of the church in Pergamum write: 'The words of him who has the sharp two-edged sword.

"'I know where you dwell, where Satan's throne is. Yet you hold fast my name, and you did not deny my faith even in the days of Antipas my faithful witness, who was killed among you, where Satan dwells. But I have a few things against you: you have some there who hold the teaching of Balaam, who taught Balak to put a stumbling block before the sons of Israel, so that they might eat food sacrificed to idols and practice sexual immorality. 15 So also you have some who hold the teaching of the Nicolaitans. 16 Therefore repent. If not, I will come to you soon and war against them with the sword of my mouth. 17 He who has an ear, let him hear what the Spirit says to the churches. To the one who conquers I will give some of the hidden manna, and I will give him a white stone, with a new name written on the stone that no one knows except the one who receives it.'

To the Church in Thyatira

"And to the angel of the church in Thyatira write: 'The words of the Son of God, who has eyes like a flame of fire, and whose feet are like burnished bronze.

"'I know your works, your love and faith and service and patient endurance, and that your latter works exceed the first. But I have this against you, that you tolerate that woman Jezebel, who calls herself a prophetess and is teaching and seducing my

servants to practice sexual immorality and to eat food sacrificed to idols. I gave her time to repent, but she refuses to repent of her sexual immorality. Behold, I will throw her onto a sickbed, and those who commit adultery with her I will throw into great tribulation, unless they repent of her works, and I will strike her children dead. And all the churches will know that I am he who searches mind and heart, and I will give to each of you according to your works. But to the rest of you in Thyatira, who do not hold this teaching, who have not learned what some call the deep things of Satan, to you I say, I do not lay on you any other burden. Only hold fast what you have until I come. The one who conquers and who keeps my works until the end, to him I will give authority over the nations, and he will rule them with a rod of iron, as when earthen pots are broken in pieces, even as I myself have received authority from my Father. And I will give him the morning star. He who has an ear, let him hear what the Spirit says to the churches.'

To the Church in Sardis

"And to the angel of the church in Sardis write: 'The words of him who has the seven spirits of God and the seven stars.

"'I know your works. You have the reputation of being alive, but you are dead. Wake up, and strengthen what remains and is about to die, for I have not found your works complete in the sight of my God. Remember, then, what you received and heard. Keep it, and repent. If you will not wake up, I will come like a

thief, and you will not know at what hour I will come against you. Yet you have still a few names in Sardis, people who have not soiled their garments, and they will walk with me in white, for they are worthy. The one who conquers will be clothed thus in white garments, and I will never blot his name out of the book of life. I will confess his name before my Father and before his angels. He who has an ear, let him hear what the Spirit says to the churches.'

To the Church in Philadelphia

"And to the angel of the church in Philadelphia write: *'The words of the holy one, the true one, who has the key of David, who opens and no one will shut, who shuts and no one opens.*

"'I know your works. Behold, I have set before you an open door, which no one is able to shut. I know that you have but little power, and yet you have kept my word and have not denied my name. Behold, I will make those of the synagogue of Satan who say that they are Jews and are not, but lie—behold, I will make them come and bow down before your feet and they will learn that I have loved you. Because you have kept my word about patient endurance, I will keep you from the hour of trial that is coming on the whole world, to try those who dwell on the earth. I am coming soon. Hold fast what you have, so that no one may seize your crown. The one who conquers, I will make him a pillar in the temple of my God. Never shall he go out of it, and I will write on him the name of my God, and the name of the city of my

Chapter 9

God, the new Jerusalem, which comes down from my God out of heaven, and my own new name. He who has an ear, let him hear what the Spirit says to the churches.'

To the Church in Laodicea

"And to the angel of the church in Laodicea write: 'The words of the Amen, the faithful and true witness, the beginning of God's creation.

"'I know your works: you are neither cold nor hot. Would that you were either cold or hot! So, because you are lukewarm, and neither hot nor cold, I will spit you out of my mouth. For you say, I am rich, I have prospered, and I need nothing, not realizing that you are wretched, pitiable, poor, blind, and naked. I counsel you to buy from me gold refined by fire, so that you may be rich, and white garments so that you may clothe yourself and the shame of your nakedness may not be seen, and salve to anoint your eyes, so that you may see. Those whom I love, I reprove and discipline, so be zealous and repent. Behold, I stand at the door and knock. If anyone hears my voice and opens the door, I will come in to him and eat with him, and he with me. The one who conquers, I will grant him to sit with me on my throne, as I also conquered and sat down with my Father on his throne. He who has an ear, let him hear what the Spirit says to the churches.'"
Revelation 2:1-3:22 ESV

Knowing Jesus as the Messiah is the initial recognition of any of his positions in the Kingdom, because without receiving him as the

Savior, we will never be able to receive him as Lord, King, or as the quickening spirit. Our reception of these quickenings are most important in understanding the realm of God's predestined and predetermined will and our provisions of conditions. Knowing Jesus as the quickening spirit gives us access to the prophetic word more fully in our lives. Unless we appreciate his desire and ability to quicken us into fullness of life, we will never respond to God's leadings into the prophetic word appropriately. This is not some far off thing, but is the result of being covered in the precious blood of Jesus that speaks greater things that that of Abel.

> *"Truly, truly, I say to you, whoever believes in me will also do the works that I do; and greater works than these will he do, because I am going to my Father." John 14:12 ESV*

Again, knowing Jesus as the quickening spirit who anoints us with power alongside the Holy Spirit, we too can learn to receive prophetic utterances and deliver them in due season through the ministry of the Spirit. As we learn to be led by the Holy Spirit, many will come to know Jesus in power through the ways we are led to minister to them. Whether that is through teaching, prophecy, healing, or even miracles, the power of Christ is available for us to access for the spreading of the Gospel, under the condition that we are willing to be used in power. Wherever there is power, there will be persecution, but wherever there is persecution for his sake, there will be quickening power to strengthen us.

The Holy Spirit has been poured out in order that we might be baptized in power, drenched in his strength and might. In the midst of this power, we must learn to be quickened in moments of divine inspiration. Remember, he told us that he would not leave us as orphans, but that he would come to us so that we would be endued with power from on high. We will never be able to spread the Gospel in every nation without receiving constant increase of spiritual power. If we expect to be able to minister effectively in the flesh, and by natural means of knowledge and wisdom, we will always find ourselves incapable. Yet, if we will recognize and walk in the spiritual power made available to us, we will see nations changed.

"Blessed are the poor in spirit, for theirs is the kingdom of heaven." Matthew 5:3 ESV

To be poor in spirit is to be in a state of personal spiritual bankruptcy. This does not mean that we mope around spiritually immature and weak, but that we are in recognition of the fact that we will never be able to do anything for God without his help. Without recognizing that we are insufficient in our own spiritual aptitude, we might easily get stuck in pride or legalism instead of learning to lean on the power and strength of Christ! No matter how big or how small the task at hand is, without Christ we are incapable of doing anything well. Being so poor in spirit that everything we gain comes as a result of begging God for mercy and help is the path to true spiritual health and hunger! Being poor in spirit allows us to be able to inherit all things, because we ourselves have nothing.

Consider the Old Testament prophets. None of them were able to speak prophetically without being anointed to do so. As I mentioned earlier, we see this depicted in a unique phrase: "The hand of the Lord came upon him." What does it mean for the hand of the Lord to come upon someone? First, let's look at a few examples of this phrase.

"But now bring me a musician." And when the musician played, the hand of the LORD came upon him." 2 Kings 3:15 ESV

"The word of the LORD came to Ezekiel the priest, the son of Buzi, in the land of the Chaldeans by the Chebar canal, and the hand of the LORD was upon him there." Ezekiel 1:3 ESV

In the same way that these saints of old were incapable of operating in spiritual strength without God's help, we too can do nothing apart from Christ. If we are truly in Christ, as Christ is in the Father, then we will set our hearts to do nothing apart from him.

"So Jesus said to them, "Truly, truly, I say to you, the Son can do nothing of his own accord, but only what he sees the Father doing. For whatever the Father does, that the Son does likewise. For the Father loves the Son and shows him all that he himself is doing. And greater works than these will he show him, so that you may marvel. For as the Father raises the dead and gives them life, so also the Son gives life to whom he will." John 5:19-21 ESV

10
Jesus as King

Jesus is not only the king of the Jews, but is also the King of Heaven and Earth. All authority in heaven and on earth has been given to him, and because of his redemptive work on the cross, his rule is everlasting. Specifically, Jesus is the King of kings in the kingdom of God. To better understand how he reigns as king, we need to understand what the kingdom is.

In Greek, the word "kingdom" is "*basilea*," which describes the right or permission granted to rule over a kingdom in royal power and dominion. Because he is the King of kings, this word also describes the royal power and dignity conferred on Christians in the Messiah's kingdom. Because we are in relationship with the King of glory who asked the Father that we might reign with him from where he is seated, we have the opportunity and privilege to walk in the authority of the King, as ambassadors and sons of the Kingdom. Therefore, knowing Jesus as Messiah is the gateway to entering into salvation. Knowing Jesus as the quickening spirit empowers us to minister in strength and power. Knowing Jesus as the King permits us to rule and reign with him as co-heirs in the kingdom of God. Because of this, we are made able to rule with dominion over the territories we are sent into.

To better appreciate why we have also been given authority to reign with Christ, we must first realize our positions in the kingdom of God. Not only are we named to be those who inherit salvation and power, but we are also called to adoption as sons and daughters that we might inherit all that belongs to our Father. Sonship is the relationship with God that allows us to rule and reign with Christ. This position we hold in the kingdom not only allows us to rule and reign outwardly as ambassadors in the kingdom of heaven, but it also permits us to access the bread that is on the King's table. Sons and Daughters of the Most High God have access to the bread that sits on the Kings table. Let's catch this revelation deep within our spirits!

Jesus said that man does not live by bread alone, but by every word that comes from the mouth of God. That descriptive statement given in the wilderness after Jesus had been fasting for 40 days and nights prophetically fulfills the typology given through the provision and gathering of the "manna" in Exodus. In Exodus, the Israelites gathered "daily bread" in order to stay fulfilled bodily while travelling in the wilderness. As Sons and Daughters of God who have been ransomed out of the world and delivered from the molestations of the enemy, we should be, like the Israelites, relying on God for our daily sustenance, going to him to gather everything we need to survive. If we will learn to do this, we will become incredible ambassadors for the kingdom, and will accomplish incredible works for Christ before his return!

> *"So then, brothers, we are debtors, not to the flesh, to live according to the flesh. For if you live according to the flesh you will die, but if by the Spirit you put to death the deeds of the body, you will live. For all who are led by the Spirit of God are sons of God. For you did not receive the spirit of slavery to fall back into fear, but you have received the Spirit of adoption as sons, by whom we cry, "Abba! Father!" The Spirit himself bears witness with our spirit that we are children of God, and if children, then heirs—heirs of God and fellow heirs with Christ, provided we suffer with him in order that we may also be glorified with him."*
> Romans 8:12-17 ESV

We should always honor Jesus as the King of heaven and earth, following his lead in all that we seek to accomplish. The most important aspect of serving our King is that we have the ability to share in the provisions of the kingdom as Sons and Daughters of the same Abba Father. Knowing that we have been justified in Christ by faith is only the beginning of understanding our roles in the kingdom of God. Our freedom from sin through the propitiation of the blood is only the beginning of our journey! Our deliverance is only the exit from Egypt, but it is not the fullness of joy, nor the fullness of the promise that we will receive when our obedience is complete. When we learn to listen, and consistently obey the words of our King, then we will experience the Kingdom of God on the earth today!

The kingdom itself is righteousness, joy, and peace in the Holy Spirit (Romans 14:17). Is joy necessary in heaven? No! Joy does its most successful work in those who experience hardships. There will be no hardships to experience in heaven. We experience them now amidst the fall of man and the presence of Satan, fallen angels, and the demonic. Peace is, likewise, a provision that is to be manifested in our lives now, before Jesus returns. If peace were something to be received when Jesus returns, he would not have been able to send the disciples out to preach the "Gospel of Peace" with the teaching he gave them. He told them to let their peace go out from them. If it remained on the people, they were told to stay, and if it returned to them, they were to dust off their feet and continue ministering throughout the cities. Without present peace, this would not have been possible. Righteousness is also to be experienced now. Righteousness has already been fulfilled in Christ through his life and his sacrifice for all sin on the cross. When we apply our faith to the reception of the Gospel message, we receive his righteousness, and it manifests in order to become an evident reality and fruit of our salvation even now on the earth.

Therefore, this idea that we are "saved" now and have to wait to enter the kingdom of God when Christ returns is a false understanding of the Kingdom of God! The kingdom itself has already come in fullness! The provisions of the kingdom are only unnoticed when we consciously choose to neglect experiencing them, blinded by the veil that is woven in lies and put over our eyes through false teachings.

What are we to do with this knowledge? Is the knowledge of a currently manifesting kingdom a provision that exists specifically for developing pure, personal spirituality? Has the kingdom come so that we might reign in life with Christ over our personal circumstances?

I believe we are made able by Christ to reign in three primary spheres of influence. Those spheres are that of our personal lives, the ministry of Jesus, and our jurisdictions and mandates.

In our personal lives, we are to reign with Christ over sin and death.

> "Therefore, since we have been justified by faith, we have peace with God through our Lord Jesus Christ. Through him we have also obtained access by faith into this grace in which we stand, and we rejoice in hope of the glory of God. Not only that, but we rejoice in our sufferings, knowing that suffering produces endurance, and endurance produces character, and character produces hope, and hope does not put us to shame, because God's love has been poured into our hearts through the Holy Spirit who has been given to us.
>
> For while we were still weak, at the right time Christ died for the ungodly. For one will scarcely die for a righteous person—though perhaps for a good person one would dare even to die—but God shows his love for us in that while we were still sinners, Christ died for us. Since, therefore, we have now been justified by his blood, much more shall we be saved by him from the wrath of God. For if while we were enemies we were reconciled to God by the death of his Son, much more, now that we are reconciled, shall we be saved by his life. More than that, we also rejoice in God through our Lord Jesus Christ, through whom we have now received reconciliation.
>
> Therefore, just as sin came into the world through one man, and death through sin, and so death spread to all men because all sinned—for sin indeed was in the world before the law was given, but sin is not counted where there is no law. Yet death reigned from Adam to Moses, even over those whose sinning was not like the transgression of Adam, who was a type of the one who was

Chapter 10

to come.

But the free gift is not like the trespass. For if many died through one man's trespass, much more have the grace of God and the free gift by the grace of that one man Jesus Christ abounded for many. And the free gift is not like the result of that one man's sin. For the judgment following one trespass brought condemnation, but the free gift following many trespasses brought justification. For if, because of one man's trespass, death reigned through that one man, much more will those who receive the abundance of grace and the free gift of righteousness reign in life through the one man Jesus Christ.

Therefore, as one trespass led to condemnation for all men, so one act of righteousness leads to justification and life for all men. For as by the one man's disobedience the many were made sinners, so by the one man's obedience the many will be made righteous. Now the law came in to increase the trespass, but where sin increased, grace abounded all the more, so that, as sin reigned in death, grace also might reign through righteousness leading to eternal life through Jesus Christ our Lord." Romans 5 ESV

"For if we have been united with him in a death like his, we shall certainly be united with him in a resurrection like his. We know that our old self was crucified with him in order that the body of sin might be brought to nothing, so that we would no longer be enslaved to sin. For one who has died has been set free from sin. Now if we have died with Christ, we believe that we

> *will also live with him. We know that Christ, being raised from the dead, will never die again; death no longer has dominion over him. For the death he died he died to sin, once for all, but the life he lives he lives to God. So you also must consider yourselves dead to sin and alive to God in Christ Jesus."* Romans 6:5-11 ESV

Because of the free gift of righteousness granted to us by our righteous King Jesus, we are able to rule over the powers of sin and death in this world. Even now, before being totally glorified in our coming resurrection bodies, we are made able through Christ's justification to reign as conquerors over our former natures. We were born into lifestyles of naturally occurring sin and death, but in the kingdom, we are set apart from sin and death to accomplish the ministry of the King. Sin in all forms had previously kept us from attaining the fullness of righteousness, peace, and joy. Now that we have entered into the kingdom of our God, through having received salvation from the Messiah and the Spirit of God in baptism, we have been given the grace and power in the Holy Spirit to experience true righteousness, peace and joy.

We have become righteous through the provisions made by Jesus on the cross. We have received peace through our faith in the Gospel of peace, and the promise of eternal salvation. We have received joy in as much as we experience the work of the Holy Spirit in our lives and through the love of our King. The power of these free gifts is that which enables us to reign with Christ in life over any obstacle that is laid before us.

> *"What then shall we say to these things? If God is for us, who can be against us? He who did not spare his own Son but gave him up for us all, how will he not also with him graciously give us all things? Who shall bring any charge against God's elect? It is God who justifies. Who is to condemn? Christ Jesus is the one who died—more than that, who was raised—who is at the right hand of God, who indeed is interceding for us. Who shall separate us from the love of Christ? Shall tribulation, or distress, or persecution, or famine, or nakedness, or danger, or sword? As it is written,*
>
> *"For your sake we are being killed all the day long; we are regarded as sheep to be slaughtered."*
>
> *No, in all these things we are more than conquerors through him who loved us. For I am sure that neither death nor life, nor angels nor rulers, nor things present nor things to come, nor powers, nor height nor depth, nor anything else in all creation, will be able to separate us from the love of God in Christ Jesus our Lord." Romans 8:31-39 ESV*

In ministry, we have been given the gifts of the Spirit.

These gifts enable the manifestations the power of the kingdom of God available to the hearts and minds of people all over the earth.

This ministry of the King is as active today as it was when it began, and possibly even more so, regardless of the doctrines we have been given that teach otherwise. Of course, Jesus, himself, appointed a strategic order to ministry in order that by following it, we might become fully mature in him. The church we see in operation today is not mature in Christ. In fact, many who claim Christ's identity look nothing like him. Instead, they bear the image and likeness of the fallen man. We cannot expect to bring a transformative Gospel to the nations if we live under the false assumption that we are incapable of living triumphant lives.

If we continue to "rest" in the lazy identities of the fallen man, we will never step into the fullness of our calling. We are not sinners saved by grace! We were sinners, who have become saints (Holy ones), who are being equipped for works of service. Those of us who have already been equipped for works of service through impartation and spiritual training in the things of the Spirit should not neglect the identity crisis that most so-called believers walk in! Instead, as ministers, we should come alongside those believers who have not yet received a comprehension of their kingdom identity. Through mature correction, and in love, we can bring others to the fullness of the stature of Christ, equipped for works of service.

"I therefore, a prisoner for the Lord, urge you to walk in a

Chapter 10

manner worthy of the calling to which you have been called, with all humility and gentleness, with patience, bearing with one another in love, eager to maintain the unity of the Spirit in the bond of peace. There is one body and one Spirit—just as you were called to the one hope that belongs to your call— one Lord, one faith, one baptism, one God and Father of all, who is over all and through all and in all. But grace was given to each one of us according to the measure of Christ's gift. Therefore it says,

"When he ascended on high he led a host of captives, and he gave gifts to men."

(In saying, "He ascended," what does it mean but that he had also descended into the lower regions, the earth? He who descended is the one who also ascended far above all the heavens, that he might fill all things.) And he gave the apostles, the prophets, the evangelists, the shepherds and teachers, to equip the saints for the work of ministry, for building up the body of Christ, until we all attain to the unity of the faith and of the knowledge of the Son of God, to mature manhood, to the measure of the stature of the fullness of Christ, so that we may no longer be children, tossed to and fro by the waves and carried about by every wind of doctrine, by human cunning, by craftiness in deceitful schemes. Rather, speaking the truth in love, we are to grow up in every way into him who is the head, into Christ, from whom the whole body, joined and held together by every joint with which it is equipped, when each part is working properly, makes the body grow so that it builds itself up in love." Ephesians 4:1-16 ESV

The five-fold ministry is that of the apostles, prophets, evangelists, pastors, and teachers. Each of these ministry positions is strategic to the building up of the body of Christ, as well as to bringing us all into unity in the knowledge of the Son of God, to mature manhood, to the measure of the stature of the fullness of Christ. Because much of the church has neglected the necessity of these gifts, we have been carried to and fro by many different winds of doctrine, by human cunning, and by craftiness in deceitful schemes. Obviously enough, we have an apparent need in the church to be brought back into the original ministry order that the King had set up when he ascended and sent the Holy Spirit to minister in his absence.

We have all been given an assignment from God, a predestined collection of works set apart for us that we might walk in them. However, many believers do not know who they were destined to be in the body of Christ. Those who do not know their places will never be able to fulfill their callings!

If we will come to know Jesus personally as our King, we can come to realize what it is he who called each of us into specifically and uniquely. These gifts are what the King desires to give to the church and to the world from the kingdom of God, ambassadors like you and me who have been called to reign with Christ in the earth. If we will seek the King for his orders and assignments for our lives, we

Chapter 10

can learn to walk in the dominion and authority that we have been equipped with to reign for him in his ongoing ministry of power, dominion, and the manifested rule of the kingdom of heaven.

Before Jesus ascended, he brought his disciples together to appoint them apostles to the church. The Word says that he breathed on each one of them saying "receive the Holy Spirit." This was not the baptism of the Holy Spirit, but the time in which the disciples received the quickening spirit of Christ for the purpose of reigning in the kingdom while he himself was to be seated at the right hand of the Father in heaven.

> *"On the evening of that day, the first day of the week, the doors being locked where the disciples were for fear of the Jews, Jesus came and stood among them and said to them, "Peace be with you." When he had said this, he showed them his hands and his side. Then the disciples were glad when they saw the Lord. Jesus said to them again, "Peace be with you. As the Father has sent me, even so I am sending you." And when he had said this, he breathed on them and said to them, "Receive the Holy Spirit. If you forgive the sins of any, they are forgiven them; if you withhold forgiveness from any, it is withheld.""* John 20:19-23 ESV

I personally believe that this is when the disciples went from being students to being ministers. In other words, this is when the disciples became apostles. The Word here tells us that Jesus gave them authority to forgive sins or withhold forgiveness from people. That is something that, previously, only God could do. In fact, to many this would be understood as blasphemy! However, we are co-heirs with Christ, sons and daughters of the same Abba Father! God, himself, has given us authority and sent us to proclaim the gospel of the kingdom with signs and wonders accompanying the truth in our message. This type of authority can only be carried by those who have a personal relationship and assignment from the King, and who have been sent by him to do the work of the kingdom of God.

The gifts that each of us have been predetermined to walk in are only able to manifest in our lives as we submit to the rule of the King who supplies our needs. Knowing him and trusting his rule is vital to ministry. This is why some pastors and teachers are able to speak directly into our personal situation through a sermon or teaching. When ministers of God get their specific ministry assignments from the king, the kingdom of God is brought forth into the light in the forms of righteousness, joy, and peace. When those who are known as ministers of God neglect to receive their assignment from the King, the teaching, sermon, or other actions taken will end up being carried out without the power of the kingdom behind them.

Why would any minister of God want to minister without power? Is it considered by some to be immature to want to minister with power? Today, I can think of many ministers who neglect the power of the Holy Spirit under the presumption that Spirit-filled ministers are seeking attention or are somehow misled in their thinking. It's not surprising that the ones who mock charismatic ministry are the same "preachers" who typically speak from their own naturally acquired knowledge of the Word, instead of the seasonal manna given from the King as needed. Their congregations are still full of people, but the people are usually not fully alive. Instead, they are luke-warm supporters who look like, smell like, and act like the world. They claim to be Christians, but live unholy lifestyles and only choose to look "religious" when it suits themselves in how they wish to be seen. Preaching the Gospel without power is like selling a car without a battery. It can look functional and capable, feel comfortable and reliable, but it will never actually run without the battery. Likewise, a Christian can look the part all day long, but until one receives power, their ministry is fruitless.

It is important that we learn from men and women who are in relationship with the King, so that what we are being taught lines up with the times and seasons that we live in on the earth today. Without this type of spiritual alignment coming from our leaders, or from the Lord himself, we will not be able to overcome the trials that come at us in each season. Remember, God has predestined times and seasons, and he has predetermined that his people would be given the provisions needed to overcome what is before us, but it is up to our leaders and ourselves to meet the conditions given by the King in each of those times. A season might last a day, a week, or even months at a time. Regardless of the length or purpose for each season of our lives, the King is always willing and ready to guide us through. He has not abandoned us to live aimlessly, but has made a way for us to connect directly with him to receive mercy and grace in time of need at the throne of Grace.

> *"Let us then with confidence draw near to the throne of grace, that we may receive mercy and find grace to help in time of need."* Hebrews 4:16 ESV

Notice again, that this access to the throne of grace (where Christ is seated at the right hand of the Father), has been made available to us in our specific time of need. We know that there is not merely one time of need that has existed between the time of his resurrection and now, but that we all experience new times of need on a constant basis. Hebrews 4 reminds us to strive to enter into his spiritual rest, approaching the throne of grace on the day that he set apart, calling it "Today." We should be striving to enter into his rest and encounter the King every day.

Chapter 10

Reigning Over Spheres of Influence

The times and places we live in are ever increasing in wickedness. People are full of deceit, living for themselves or worshipping idols that will never grant them salvation. Fortunately, we have the opportunity to live in the same geographical territory as these people. We work with them, our children go to school with them, and most of us have probably been just like these people at some point in our lives. It is good that we have the opportunity to live amongst those who neglect the need for a righteous Messiah, Spirit, King, and Lord. It is why we have not been removed from the earth! If there was no need to spread the good news of Christ, each of us would have been raptured as soon as we believed on him!

What we need to recognize is that people who have not yet called upon the Lord are being led by the same spiritual influences that we were following before we met Jesus. The reason that people live in such a wicked way is not because they were created wicked, but because they are under the influence of their father, the devil. Not only that, but the presence of evil is abundant around them. Many have either knowingly or unknowingly come into covenants with the demonic, or are under the rule of principalities.

We live under the rule of a righteous King because we know him, and have submitted to him. Those who do not know the King, and who have not chosen to enter the kingdom, are living under the rule of the fallen angels who still rule over many kingdoms of the world. We also were under that rule previously, and lived in ways that very easily represented the kingdom of darkness that took precedent rule over us.

"And you were dead in trespasses and sins in which you walked, following the course of this world, following the prince of the power of the air, the spirit that is now at work in the sons of disobedience – among whom we all once lived in the passions of our flesh, carrying out the desires of the body and the mind, and were by nature children of wrath, like the rest of mankind. But God, being rich in mercy, because of the great love with which he loved us, even when we were dead in our trespasses, made us alive together with Christ – by grace you have been saved – and raised up with him and seated us with him in the heavenly places in Christ Jesus, so that in the coming ages he might show the immeasurable riches of his grace in kindness toward us in Christ Jesus." Ephesians 2:1-7 ESV

We have been saved from these adulterous ways set up against God, not because we earned it, but because God is merciful and kind to those who love him! However, that means we have work to do! We weren't saved so that we could live for ourselves, but so that we could live like Christ, who obviously lived his life for the sake of the world. What part do we have to play in these times and in these regions where we live? If Jesus has been given all authority and power over the world, we are to be working in his authority to battle in spirit against these forces of evil. That being said, we need to understand how spiritual warfare works, so that we don't get in a battle whereby we do not become overcomers. Jesus has already won the war for us, but it's up to us to overcome the enemy personally and corporately in battles of regional warfare in order to experience the fullness of what he did for us on the cross.

The cross of Christ is sufficient for salvation, but salvation alone does not provide every believer with total victory over all battles of life. It is by the power of the message of the cross that we choose to battle. In other words, Jesus' sacrifice on the cross is only as powerful as it is appropriated in our daily lives. If we choose to rest on our own successes instead of the victory won on the cross, we will experience failure in spiritual battle. In those times of failure, we might even enter into a battle fatigue, where our awareness of the cross is only a vague suggestion, but never the answer to the spiritual problem.

"Therefore, having this ministry by the mercy of God, we do not lose heart. But we have renounced disgraceful, underhanded ways. We refuse to practice cunning or to tamper with God's word, but by the open statement of the truth we would commend ourselves to everyone's conscience in the sight of God. And even

if our gospel is veiled, it is veiled to those who are perishing. In their case the god of this world has blinded the minds of the unbelievers, to keep them from seeing the light of the gospel of the glory of Christ, who is the image of God. For what we proclaim is not ourselves, but Jesus Christ as Lord, with ourselves as your servants for Jesus' sake. For God, who said, "Let light shine out of darkness," has shone in our hearts to give the light of the knowledge of the glory of God in the face of Jesus Christ.

But we have this treasure in jars of clay, to show that the surpassing power belongs to God and not to us. We are afflicted in every way, but not crushed; perplexed, but not driven to despair; persecuted, but not forsaken; struck down, but not destroyed; always carrying in the body the death of Jesus, so that the life of Jesus may also be manifested in our bodies. For we who live are always being given over to death for Jesus' sake, so that the life of Jesus also may be manifested in our mortal flesh. So death is at work in us, but life in you.

Since we have the same spirit of faith according to what has been written, "I believed, and so I spoke," we also believe, and so we also speak, knowing that he who raised the Lord Jesus will raise us also with Jesus and bring us with you into his presence. For it is all for your sake, so that as grace extends to more and more people it may increase thanksgiving, to the glory of God.

So we do not lose heart. Though our outer self is wasting away, our inner self is being renewed day by day. For this light momentary affliction is preparing for us an eternal weight of glory beyond all comparison, as we look not to the things that are seen but to the things that are unseen. For the things that are seen are transient, but the things that are unseen are eternal." 2 Corinthians 4:1-18 ESV

The fact is that we will inevitably suffer for our faith, even physically, but we should never have to suffer spiritually. Our spirituality should never falter as a result of any attack because we have been joined with the Holy Spirit! God will quicken us into life by his Spirit that is within us so that we can endure any hardships with supernatural joy and comfort. We will face the trials that come against us in this life as we bring light into the darkness and expose the lies in the midst of the knowledge of truth. We have been given power as a result of the work Christ accomplished on the cross.

"For the weapons of our warfare are not of the flesh but have divine power to destroy strongholds. We destroy arguments and every lofty opinion raised against the knowledge of God, and take every thought captive to obey Christ, being ready to punish every disobedience, when your obedience is complete." 2 Corinthians 10:4-6 ESV

"Finally, be strong in the Lord and in the strength of his might. Put on the whole armor of God, that you may be able to stand against the schemes of the devil. For we do not wrestle against flesh and blood, but against the rulers, against the authorities,

against the cosmic powers over this present darkness, against the spiritual forces of evil in the heavenly places." Ephesians 6:10-12 ESV

Because we have been seated with Christ at the right hand of the Father in heavenly places, we have authority to rule and reign with him over the presence of darkness at work in the world today. Yet because we are seated "with" him, we can only work as he leads us. We are not seated on the throne by ourselves, with authority to rule and reign as we please, but we are seated with him. We must always seek to know what our King is giving us authority to do in these times and seasons in which we live.

I do believe that Jesus gives each of us specific authority to rule and reign over the powers of darkness at work around us, but I also believe that it is specific to his own will. Of course, we need to understand what it means to rule and reign over darkness. We have already been given authority to heal the sick, cast out demons, and preach the Gospel of the kingdom. We have already been commissioned to carry out the Great Commission and make disciples of nations. Yet, those are only the foundations of what we have been given authority to do.

11
Warring Under the King

In order to explain our roles in regional spiritual warfare under the rule of King Jesus, I want to share 5 major steps of warfare that I believe are mandatory to follow. We do not battle against the enemies of darkness in any region as we please, because we were never given authority to function independently from Jesus. Instead, we use the authority we have been given to overwhelm the kingdoms of darkness in specific regions that we are sent to and for specific purposes. These steps will help us understand what questions we should be asking when entering into regional warfare under the rule of our King Jesus.

Know that you are sent!

Know the time and season that you are sent.

Know the Purpose for why you are sent.

Prove through factual information the regional strongholds.

Bind and Plunder.

Know that you are sent!

Knowing whether or not we might even need to be sent into specific regions to manifest the rule of our King has everything to do with recognizing the need for apostolic ministry in the church today. If there were no need for apostolic ministry, Jesus would have clearly instructed us about the end of an apostolic age or a ceasing of that anointing, but thankfully he never did!

Depending on where we are sent to minister, we will have to face specific strongholds over regions and specific forces of darkness. The spiritual issues that we might face in America will be much different than those that are faced in places like India or China. Our ability to perceive what we might face in new territories is subject to our ability to receive instruction from the King. That means that we are only as effective as we are dependent on him. We cannot expect to be able to quickly overthrow the Dominions in regions on our own, but only when we have received specific intel regarding what actually exists there during the season of its uprooting. Believe it or not, specific territories across the earth deal with specific demonic activity, principalities and powers of the air.

In Daniel, we learn that there was a dark prince reigning with Satan over the kingdom of Persia. This principality waged war against the angel God had sent to deliver breakthrough to Daniel in his time of prayer and fasting. Because he persisted in prayer without giving up on God's faithfulness, the prince was defeated in a battle against Michael the Archangel. When this entity was defeated, Daniel received the breakthrough for which he had been praying.

There are prayer warriors all over the world right now praying for breakthrough in areas of their lives, in the life of the church, and in the life of the nations. We should always expect that there are forces of evil at work against their prayers. When we go to minister in any region or to any people, we should always seek the King for instruction on how to deal with what forces are at work against the people. Specifically, it would be incredibly important to find out what is being prayed for! What are the people of the nation or people group believing for? When we receive that information and the consequent instruction from the King regarding those things, we can carry out his administration of the kingdom to help bring about whatever it is he intends to do with the people. I will add a very important point to this topic: our primary focus should always be to remain in Christ, abiding in his words, and refraining from all kinds of sin and darkness. It is with clean hands and pure hearts that we will minister, so that we do not hinder ourselves from being effective in the process.

I believe that we live in one of the most crucial times in human history. We face some of the most brutal attacks of the enemy against our people, both in the church and in the nations. Because we can only expect for things to get worse as they get better, we will need to rely on God to deliver unprecedented levels of knowledge and power to us in these times so that we might be effective in demolishing the stronghold over the regions we are sent into. We do not wage war against the flesh, but against the powers of evil in spiritual realms. I believe God will be pouring out knowledge and wisdom to those who seek him for the purpose of reaching every nation with the Gospel of Christ. Along with an increase of knowledge and power comes responsibility. If we will learn to be mature with God's work and Word, we will be those who God empowers to overcome the darkness on behalf of others. We will be the recipients of the knowledge needed to prevail.

"And it shall come to pass afterward, that I will pour out my Spirit on all flesh; your sons and your daughters shall prophesy,

Chapter 11

your old men shall dream dreams, and your young men shall see visions." Joel 2:28 ESV

Throughout the Bible (both in the Old Testament and in the New) whenever God gave new knowledge and wisdom to his people, he often did so through dreams, visions, and the prophetic word. We see this with all of the prophets and mighty men and women of God in the Old and New Testaments. In fact, the only other form by which God gave unprecedented levels of knowledge, wisdom, authority, and power was through the person of Jesus Christ, his Son, while he ministered on the earth. I believe God is still in the business of revealing his predestined and predetermined will through dreams, visions, and prophecy. I am deeply convicted by the fact that we will need them to overcome what we must endure as we await the return of our King. I also believe that the lands of the earth can be stabilized by the few who will seek these things out in purity and righteousness. Just as God would have kept from destroying Sodom and Gomorrah if there were only ten righteous in the land, I believe that our obedience to him can keep the stability of a land intact.

"The wicked flee when no one pursues, but the righteous are bold as a lion. When a land transgresses, it has many rulers, but with a man of understanding and knowledge, its stability will long continue." Proverbs 28:1-2 ESV

> *"If my people who are called by my name humble themselves, and pray and seek my face and turn from their wicked ways, then I will hear from heaven and will forgive their sin and heal their land. Now my eyes will be open and my ears attentive to the prayer that is made in this place. For now I have chosen and consecrated this house that my name may be there forever. My eyes and my heart will be there for all time. And as for you, if you will walk before me as David your father walked, doing according to all that I have commanded you and keeping my statutes and my rules, then I will establish your royal throne, as I covenanted with David your father, saying, 'You shall not lack a man to rule Israel.'" 2 Chronicles 7:14-18 ESV*

God is calling us to be a people who will live for him and seek his face. If we will do this, I believe that God will pour out upon us new knowledge and wisdom and power, revealing to us the work of the enemy in the nations. We will be given knowledge of the presence and power of strongholds set up in the lands. These strongholds can only be uprooted after the repentance of a people. However, many do not recognize the need for repentance. For those who will harken to his voice, he will grant to see the work of lawlessness in these lands.

We must be willing to be shown what is taking place, and must be willing to embrace these battles as ambassadors of repentance. The legal rights that the enemy has against the nations must be repented of and renounced. Many have entered into wickedness by the leading of the enemy, and have never repented for their works. It is up to the people of God, those who reign with the King, to humbly repent and renounce any dealings with the enemy on behalf of the people. We must turn our backs on sin, transgressions, iniquities, and covenants with the demonic.

By doing so, we will expose the wickedness before God on the earth and in the presence of the people of these lands. God desires to pour out his forgiveness to those who will embrace it through knowing his Son, Jesus. When we have removed the strongholds from these regions, we will need to plunder the house. This means that we carry the burdens of the people to the only one who can bear the burdens of a nation, our King Jesus. If we will do this work, I believe God will bring restoration to these nations, and the power of the Gospel of Christ will be able to reach the inhabitants of those lands with quickness. We have the opportunity to see millions of lives saved by the power of God. Are we willing to reign with the King?

Know the time and season that you are sent.

In the same way that police officers have a jurisdiction, ministers and saints in the kingdom of God who are sent into regions to do warfare have specific authority that is only relevant to the jurisdiction to which they are sent. The one who sends is the one who give the jurisdiction and the authority to enforce justice in those places.

Know the Purpose for why you are sent.

God will not send you into trials, sufferings, successes, or breakthroughs without purpose. There is a purpose of God on everyone's life. The opportunity we have to inquire of the Lord to find out what those purposes are is unparalleled, but often warred against. The enemy wants you to be so distracted from your purpose that you abandon your assignment altogether to pursue something that doesn't line up with the provision of God for the season.

Prove through factual information the regional strongholds.

Don't just go into regions to wage warfare under an impression that someone gave you about a stronghold or issue. First, find the proof. Some regions have racial strongholds because of a history of racial hate or tension in the region. When you can prove the stronghold through what people are doing, or have done in the past, it gives you a more solid understanding of what you are dealing with as well as gives you a better perspective to release intercession from. Remember, no prophecy has ever gone forth from the will of man, but God speaks over regions through man to accomplish his prophetic will for the regions. Whenever you declare a prophetic utterance over a land in order to see a physical change in the warfare, you are actually prophesying in proportion to your faith as with the gift mentioned in Romans 12.

Bind and Plunder

The reason for regional warfare has everything to do with the glory belonging to kingdoms. Fallen angelic principalities and hosts are bent on taking glory for themselves. It's in their nature to want to gain dominion over people's possessions. From the time they fell until now, they have been trying to take glory from God. Their sights aren't just set on the rule of God or the Fatherhood of God. These fallen angels have their sights set on the glory of God!

Because we have been given rule and dominion over the kingdoms of the world, we should be actively taking spiritual territory and plundering the glory of the spiritual kingdoms of the world.

When God brought the Israelites out of Egypt, they didn't leave in rags. The Word tells us that the women and children came out of Egypt wearing fine linens, and adorned with the finest gold and jewels!

> *"The Egyptians were urgent with the people to send them out of the land in haste. For they said, "We shall all be dead." So the people took their dough before it was leavened, their kneading*

bowls being bound up in their cloaks on their shoulders. The people of Israel had also done as Moses told them, for they had asked the Egyptians for silver and gold jewelry and for clothing. And the Lord had given the people favor in the sight of the Egyptians, so that they let them have what they asked. Thus they plundered the Egyptians." Exodus 12:33-36 ESV

12
Jesus as Lord

So far, we've looked into the aspects of knowing Jesus as Messiah for the purpose of receiving salvation, knowing him in the Spirit in order to receive power, and knowing him as King so that we might rule and reign with him, having dominion over all things. All of those things are great, but can we really experience the fullness of each of their rewards without knowing Jesus as Lord? What does the word "Lord" even mean? To understand how we are to interact with Jesus as Lord, we will need to explore the answer to that question.

The Hebrew word for "lord," "*'adown*," describes the role of a master. It is used to describe various roles of authority including husbands, prophets, princes, kings, fathers, priests, theophanic angels

(angels of the Lord), or other general titles recognizing superiority. This word is separate from the word used to describe Jehovah, which is a totally capitalized word, LORD. When the word LORD is used in the Bible, it refers to God only. When the lower case is used, it can describe any person with superiority or authority over another.

In Greek, the word used to describe the Lord Jesus is *"kyrios."* This word describes the one to whom a person or a thing belongs, about which he has power of deciding, mastering, or lording over. It labels the possessor or disposer of a thing, such as an owner who has control over a person, and who decides whether or not they will obtain the possessions he himself owns. It recognizes honor expressive of respect and reverence, with which servants speak to their master. Most notably it describes the title given to God that is most common to us.

In light of the other positions Jesus holds within our relationship with him, Lord is the most demanding. It is demanding because without honoring him as Lord, we cannot receive him as Messiah, King, or the quickening Spirit. To give an example of this, we could consider the relationship between a child and a parent. The child, without first recognizing their parent as such, will not be able to fully embrace the love bestowed on them through the actions taken by parents that make them "protectors," "providers," "helpers," "teachers," or "guardians." In this example, knowing the parent as "father" or "mother" opens the child up for learning to understand the other various aspects of their parent's total identities.

Consider the Apostle Paul when he addressed the angel of the Lord that came to him while he was still living as a persecutor of the church.

"But Saul, still breathing threats and murder against the disciples of the Lord, went to the high priest and asked him for letters to the synagogues at Damascus, so that if he found any belonging to the Way, men or women, he might bring them bound to Jerusalem. Now as he went on his way, he approached Damascus, and suddenly a light from heaven shone around him. And falling to the ground, he heard a voice saying to him, "Saul, Saul, why are you persecuting me?" And he said, "Who are you, Lord?" And he said, "I am Jesus, whom you are persecuting." Acts 9:1-5 ESV

Before believing on Jesus as his Messiah, he addressed him in reverence of his authority as Lord, even without knowing his name. In the same way, when we come to know Christ as our Messiah, we need to have a deep conviction of reverence toward his authority as Lord first. The Word tells us that the fear of the Lord is the beginning of both knowledge and wisdom. It is safe to admit that the Holy and reverential fear of the Lord must always be present as a predecessor to the knowledge and wisdom we receive through it that reveals Christ's true identity as the Messiah and Savior of the world.

Jesus once asked Peter, "who do you say that I am?" When Peter replied with his answer, that Jesus was the Son of God, Jesus told him he did not come up with such idea on his own, but that it was revealed to him by the Father in heaven. Whenever Peter received this revelation, it was delivered in the form of wisdom and knowledge, as a result of the "fear of the Lord" he had learned to develop in his heart.

Before knowing and experiencing his quickening spiritual presence in our lives, and before we are made able to move in his anointing, we must first honor him as the Lord. The anointing of Christ's spirit is what works in us to bring about his power in ministering his Gospel. We do not minister by our own power, or in our own gospel. Every resource we have for ministry belongs to the Lord. Remember, a lord is a possessor and owner of something. When we recognize him as our Lord, we are submitting to his control over our lives. That means that we make a deep conscious decision to belong to him and his leadership over us. We cannot minister out of our own wills and desires and still bring about lasting change in the nations. Instead, we must submit to his Lordship over us and be quickened by his spiritual anointing to perform lasting service in the work of

Chapter 12

the kingdom.

When it comes to knowing Jesus as King, we have learned that if we join him in his rule, we are able to move in his rule and power as co-heirs and sons of God. However, every king in any kingdom is also a lord. The King of kings, likewise, is automatically the Lord of Lords. I live in the United States, which is not a kingdom, but a democracy. Our officials are elected, but owned by the people. Our elected officials only have the authority that we give them by voting them into office, and the decisions they make typically have to go through an approval process where other elected officials work together to pass legislation. That is not how a kingdom works! In the U.S., the President does not own the land, total wealth, or goods of the nation. In a kingdom, the king does own the land and everything in it. If a king makes a decision, the whole kingdom is expected to submit to his rule. Also, because the king is a possessor and owner of all that is in the kingdom, he does not have a need for an advisor. He could elect an advisor if he wants to, whereby he shares possession and counsel over the kingdom with the one whom he elects, but he is not required to consult any person before making decrees or proclamations. They can make sovereign decisions with absolute authority without being questioned.

If people decide to rebel against a king, their actions will be labeled as blasphemy against him. Punishment is then awarded to the criminal who rebelled against the king. On the other hand, whoever submits to the king and his rule is guaranteed the protection and security of the king. When we submit to the King of kings, Jesus Christ, we are covered by his own protection and security, and we receive his favor as our reward. This kingdom concept is how the rule of heaven and earth operate under the Lordship of Jesus.

Knowing Jesus as Lord is the narrow pathway to receiving salvation, power, kingdom dominion, and authority. Without submitting to him as Lord, we can have no authority. Because Christ reigns over all things in heaven and on earth, all things belong to him. Ownership, therefore, is the worst possible mindset we can come into when it comes to administrating kingdom business. When we take up a mindset of ownership with the gifts given by the king, we are actually working against the king in a form of rebellion. We do not serve an unholy or unrighteous King, but a perfect and righteous, Holy King. We should never fear his processes or decisions because all of his thoughts toward us are good. He is faithful.

This is a unique struggle with ownership that exists in serving Christ as Lord. It is vitally important for us to allow this to sink deep into our hearts! We do not own anything in the kingdom, but we steward all that has been given to us by him. Each of us hold various levels of responsibility, in accordance with the possessions that he has allowed us to share in him. Whenever we claim ownership of what we have been given to steward, our privileges will start to fail. An omniscient God who is present in all areas of our lives at all times is not going to empower kingdom ministry that is being led or operated by servants and leaders who are in disobedience with the King.

Why is that? Why would God not empower ministry? This has to do with who is receiving glory for the work we do. All glory in heaven and on earth should always be given to the Lord! We are not to be worshipped, just as we are not to worship angels. All worship belongs to Jesus our Lord. True worship is a release of glory because glory represents value. When we declare from our hearts what is most valuable to us, we release glory.

We should all strive to shower God with these valuable praises persistently, on all occasions! He is worthy of all of our praise as we glorify his name. I hope that I am able to reveal how the knowledge of the truth about the identity of Jesus brings about a truthful spirit of worship, because that is exactly what knowing him creates. When we carry hearts of worship, we bestow glory and honor on God, and develop as overcomers. That is why the enemy seeks to defeat true, spiritual worship mentalities.

Fear is the primary tactic that is used to defeat our desire to worship God. If the enemy can cause us to fear, we will inevitably begin to admit rejection toward the Lord. We honor and submit to the Lord by living lives of worship, and we reject him by living life in fear. Imagine if we were to begin fearing lack, which many call a "poverty mentality." If we fear having a lack of provision, then we are not trusting the Lord. Would anyone worship a Lord they do not trust?

Whenever we begin to feel as though we do not have enough provision to meet our needs, what we are actually doing is developing ownership mentalities. A recognition of lack infers that we somehow have formed an idea that some of what we possess actually belongs to us. Although this may seem impractical in Western civilization, those who live under the rule of King Jesus have actually given all they have to him in total surrender. We are not the owners of our possessions, but have given all things over to Christ so that he can rule and reign in our lives. We have surrendered our entire lives to him!

When we live from a mentality that says, "all I have is yours, Lord," we will never experience lack. Instead, we will learn to be stewards of all things, knowing that all we have actually belongs to him because we trust him as our Lord. Then, when there is need, we won't stress ourselves out by thinking we have to rely on our own means to provide what is needed. Instead, we will trust him who sees all things to provide all that we need. Is the God who created the heavens and the earth, who clothes the animals of the field and birds of the air (who takes care of all that we do not see) incapable of meeting every need we might have? Of course not! He is more than able to provide for us beyond what our hearts can measure.

Within this same concept, we could see how worry and anxiety are tactics of the enemy which work to remove the influence of God's provisions. By worrying, we are neglecting the opportunity we have to trust God. Is that naïve? No! The wisdom of man would tell you to worry, but the wisdom of God would say that God's ways are better, higher, and faithful! If we are anxious all the time about how things might work out, have we really submitted our hearts and cares to the Lord?

> *"Rejoice in the Lord always; again I will say, rejoice. Let your reasonableness be known to everyone. The Lord is at hand; do not be anxious about anything, but in everything by prayer and supplication with thanksgiving let your requests be made known to God. And the peace of God, which surpasses all understanding, will guard your hearts and your minds in Christ Jesus." Philippians 4:4-7 ESV*

> *"Do not lay up for yourselves treasures on earth, where moth and rust destroy and where thieves break in and steal, but lay up for yourselves treasures in heaven, where neither moth nor rust*

destroys and where thieves do not break in and steal. For where your treasure is, there your heart will be also.

"The eye is the lamp of the body. So, if your eye is healthy, your whole body will be full of light, but if your eye is bad, your whole body will be full of darkness. If then the light in you is darkness, how great is the darkness!

"No one can serve two masters, for either he will hate the one and love the other, or he will be devoted to the one and despise the other. You cannot serve God and money.

"Therefore I tell you, do not be anxious about your life, what you will eat or what you will drink, nor about your body, what you will put on. Is not life more than food, and the body more than clothing? Look at the birds of the air: they neither sow nor reap nor gather into barns, and yet your heavenly Father feeds them. Are you not of more value than they? And which of you by being anxious can add a single hour to his span of life? And why are you anxious about clothing? Consider the lilies of the field, how they grow: they neither toil nor spin, yet I tell you, even Solomon in all his glory was not arrayed like one of these. But if God so clothes the grass of the field, which today is alive and tomorrow is thrown into the oven, will he not much more clothe you, O you of little faith? Therefore do not be anxious, saying, 'What shall we eat?' or 'What shall we drink?' or 'What shall we wear?' For the Gentiles seek after all these things, and your heavenly Father knows that you need them all. But seek first the kingdom of God and his righteousness, and all these things will be added to you." Matthew 6:19-33 ESV

13
"I'm waiting for my people to trust my position."

Why do we receive convictions in our hearts? Where do they come from? Why are they important? How can these simple and spontaneous thoughts carry such heavy burdens with them?

After seeking the voice of the Father on the answers to these questions, I've begun to truly experience a new understanding of the power of the Holy Spirit in the provisions of his convictions. These three things are what the Father has spoken:

I'm waiting for my people to trust my position.

I'm ready for my people to trust my perspective.

I'm ready for my people to join me in my vineyard venture.

Each time he spoke, I also received visual pictures. One major way that the Holy Spirit reveals the Father's heart to me is through pictures, dreams, and visions. Along with his spoken words, I receive visuals. Anytime he speaks to me in these ways, I take what I've heard or seen and I dive into Scripture to see how it all unfolds. The Word of God is living and active, so anytime I get new revelation, the Bible is always able to confirm what I see and hear.

When he spoke those words to me, I was puzzled. I had no clue what he meant by his "position." I asked "What is your position?" and I began to see a picture in my mind of a sawhorse. Yes, a sawhorse! (If you have no clue what a sawhorse is, it's an "A" shaped support tool that carpenters use to lay their work on while they are cutting or making changes to the project.) I thought I was puzzled before I asked, but now I had become even more unsure of what the Lord was trying to tell me. So, I asked, "Do you have a verse for that?" He said "Of course, Psalm 37:17."

"For the arms of the wicked shall be broken, but the Lord upholds the righteous." Psalm 37:17 ESV

There it was, instantly I knew why he showed me his position as a sawhorse. God is waiting for us to trust him as the upholder of the righteous. I could see the rest of the picture unfolding. As the Holy Spirit teaches, comforts, and exhorts us into maturity and righteousness, the Lord upholds us! We are his workmanship, his craftsmanship!

The Hebrew word for "uphold" is "*camak*," and it means: to establish, refresh, and to revive to rest. It also can mean to lean, lay, or rest upon something for support. Our role in this relationship with God is to approach him, knowing that we can rest on him for support, to be revived, refreshed, and receive rest. It is so important for us to live from a place of resting in God. He is our refuge. We can find true rest only in God, all other forms of rest are counterfeits. If we think that by making six-figure salaries we will somehow find rest, we are wrong. If we think we can find rest in new homes and new cars, we are fooling ourselves. Rest is only found when we become dependent and reliant on the one, true God.

Resting on anything other than God is idolatry. Men and women all over the world today find their comfort in material things that will never satisfy them. Unfortunately, that statement is also true for many Christians. How will we ever come to know God as the upholder if we never lean on him for all that we need? We cannot! Thankfully, God has made a way for us to enter into his rest every day, through his Son Jesus.

"Come to me, all who labor and are heavy laden, and I will give you rest. Take my yoke upon you, and learn from me, for

I am gentle and lowly in heart, and you will find rest for your souls. For my yoke is easy, and my burden is light." Matthew 11:28-29 ESV

In this verse, the words "come to me" are not given as some sort of distant suggestion. They are not figurative either, meaning that this verse is not telling us to "think happy thoughts about Jesus." These words are more of a command to go to him where he is seated at the right hand of the Father, at the throne of grace. We cannot assume that by simply thinking about casting our burdens on him we have come to experience his rest. We must actually approach his throne with confidence and boldness, knowing that he is willing and able to meet our needs. Without him we will fail, but with him, we will conquer.

"So then, there remains a Sabbath rest for the people of God, for whoever has entered God's rest has also rested from his works as God did from his. Let us therefore strive to enter that rest, so that no one may fall by the same sort of disobedience. For the word of God is living and active, sharper than any two-edged sword, piercing to the division of soul and of spirit, of joints and of marrow, and discerning the thoughts and intentions of the heart. And no creature is hidden from his sight, but all are naked and exposed to the eyes of him to whom we must give account." Hebrews 4:9-13 ESV

This verse, again, is a strong exhortation to the church. We cannot live effectively as Christians without having personal encounters with God in the place of his rest. We must learn to rest from our works and lean on him to receive from him by his Word. The Word of God is only living and active when it is received. Until we rest in the personal knowledge and revelation of the Word, we will not begin to experience the division of soul and spirit, joints and marrow, nor the discernment of the thoughts and intentions of the heart. However, when we rest on him and his word, the convictions we receive by the Spirit will work in our lives to remove what doesn't belong and empower us by what does.

> *"O God, save me by your name, and vindicate me by your might. O God, hear my prayer; give ear to the words of my mouth. For strangers have risen against me; ruthless men seek my life; they do not set God before themselves. Selah. Behold, God is my helper; the Lord is the upholder of my life. He will return the evil to my enemies; in your faithfulness put an end to them. With a freewill offering I will sacrifice to you; I will give thanks to your name, O Lord, for it is good. For he has delivered me from every trouble, and my eye has looked in triumph on my enemies." Psalm 54:1-7 ESV*

Whenever we are under attack, either by physical or spiritual enemies, God is our helper. He is the one who will deliver us from the attack if we will learn to know him and trust him as the Upholder. To trust the Lord is to be confident with him. It is to have confidence in his ability to provide for us. When we trust God, we not only become vulnerable with him, but we also become bold in our speech towards him. Trust builds our relationship with God through experiencing his security. He is not careless with us, but watches over us to provide safety when we need it. When we trust God, we can learn to become fearless because we know he will always take care of us. Trusting the Lord to uphold us as we are being trained up in his ways is one of the most powerful decisions we can continually make.

> *"Create in me a clean heart, O God, and renew a right spirit within me. Cast me not away from your presence, and take not your Holy Spirit from me. Restore to me the joy of your salvation, and uphold me with a willing spirit." Psalm 51:10-12 ESV*

When we learn of his goodness, we will fear separation from it. Staying close to him becomes a necessity when we trust him. I think this cry to the Lord is so powerful because it shows how vulnerable David was willing to be with God, even though he had made horrible decisions. Before praying this prayer, he had committed adultery with Bathsheba, impregnated her, and had his friend, her husband, who was loyal to him both as a friend and as a servant, murdered on the frontlines of battle. Even though he had sinned in such horrible ways, he was willing to trust God and be vulnerable with him in this bold prayer.

We also learn in this verse that David sought God out as his upholder, "Uphold me with a willing spirit." Are we confident enough with our God to ask him to uphold us even when we are guilty of sinning against him? Are we truly willing to ask him to create in us clean hearts and renew right spirits within us, even if it means that we might be thrown in the fire to be refined? If so, we have found ourselves not only trusting in his goodness, but living dependent on his willingness to sustain us.

"Uphold me according to your promise, that I may live, and let me not be put to shame in my hope! Hold me up, that I may be safe and have regard for your statutes continually!" Psalm 119:116-117 ESV

In this verse, the psalmist is asking that God uphold him by his spoken word. The Hebrew word used for "your promise" can also be translated into "your word," and is worded that way in other translations. It is the Hebrew word "*'imrah*" which means "utterance, speech, or word." It is derived from the word "*'emer*," which can describe a promise or command. "*Emer*" comes from the root "*'amar*," which means "to say, speak, or utter in one's heart, to boast, or to act proudly."

Notice that the inference suggests that without God's spoken word, he would not be able to live in the way he desires. Without God's word, our hope would be put to shame. God's spoken word, revealed to us in our hearts, removes shame and replaces it with hope so that we can truly live. When God speaks to us continually today by the Holy Spirit, we are able to remain safe and have regard for his statutes continually.

What is a statute? In Hebrew, the word is "*choq,*" and it describes a prescribed task, portion, action, limit, boundary, law, or condition. A statute is a prescription from God, we might call it "a doctor's orders." If we will wait on the Lord daily, he will come and speak to us, and he will give us daily prescriptions to follow that will help to keep us within the boundaries of healthy spiritual life. If we are going to walk in the Spirit, we will need to continually regard his statues. God will give us our daily prescriptions!

The best way to describe practically how we can receive these prescriptions is to recognize that they are what we call "convictions." Earlier, I covered the principles of understanding God's predestined will and his predetermined will. I stated that God's predestined events always occur in specific times and seasons, and always have signs accompanying them. I wrote that God's predetermined provisions always come with conditions. These principles apply not only to the prophetic word, but also to daily life when we are walking by the Spirit.

Convictions of the Holy Spirit are actually the revelations of the conditions we need to meet in order to receive provisions from God every day. The Spirit speaks to us in many different ways, but his primary goal is to work through convictions to transform us by the renewing of our minds. Whenever a true prophet speaks regarding times and seasons, he reveals a glimpse of God's predestined will, and usually reveals the signs that will accompany those times. When we hear those types of prophetic utterances, we can be sure that they will come to pass, regardless of what we do. However, if we have a part to play in the work God has predestined to carry out, the Holy Spirit will convict us in whatever way we need to be adjusted, so that we can meet the conditions by faith and be equipped for the good works. Of course, we are not saved by these works, but the kingdom is built by them.

I am a parent, and if I knew ahead of time that a big event was going to take place in my children's lives, would I speak out to warn them and instruct them before it took place? Of course, I would! How much more will God speak to his children? That is why he sent the Holy Spirit, to encourage the children of God, and to correct us when we are getting off track so that we might come into alignment with his will in predestined times and seasons.

When God speaks, whether through personal convictions or through the ministers of the kingdom, he helps us to focus on the right things. Those who have experienced the power existing in the prophetic gifts will often seek to receive prophetic words. Yet, convictions are just as powerful and are available to us at all times. Also, if we will learn to tune in to the convictions of the Holy Spirit, and obey them, we will become more trustworthy with God's Word, and thereby may become the ministers entrusted with his prophetic utterances for others.

> *"Pursue love, and earnestly desire the spiritual gifts, especially that you may prophesy. For one who speaks in a tongue speaks not to men but to God; for no one understands him, but he utters mysteries in the Spirit. On the other hand, the one who prophesies speaks to people for their upbuilding and encouragement and consolation. The one who speaks in a tongue builds up himself, but the one who prophesies builds up the church. Now I want you all to speak in tongues, but even more to prophesy. The one who prophesies is greater than the one who speaks in tongues, unless someone interprets, so that the church may be built up." 1 Corinthians 14:1-6 ESV*

Paul encourages us to desire the greater gifts, especially prophecy, but not for our own personal benefit. Whenever we prophesy, we build up the body of Christ. There is a bit of a fine line between speaking out of our convictions, and boasting in knowledge. If anyone is speaking to the body of Christ out of a deep conviction, we need to be sure that it is not being done for self-gain, but for the building up of others. In the same way, when we meet the conditions of faith that are revealed through convictions of the Holy Spirit, and experience the provisions of God, we should never boast that we have done it in our own power. Instead, we boast in the power of grace at work in our lives.

Remaining dependent on God is the key to receiving provisions through the convictions spoken to our hearts by the Holy Spirit. Without him speaking, we are left to our own abilities, which are weak. If good things come to us as a result of being dependent on God, then he always gets the glory. If we ever come into a mindset that causes us to think that we are capable of doing good works for the kingdom by our own means, we will end up unknowingly seeking glory for ourselves to no avail. We will share in his glory in the end when he glorifies us, but until then, God deserves all the glory, and it will belong to him.

Exhortations are provided when God lets one of us reveal convictions to others so that they are able to meet God's conditions. It would be like a nurse bringing in a signed prescription document at the doctor's office. The nurse did not write the prescription, but only delivered it. The doctor wrote it and signed it, but allowed it to be delivered to the patient by the nurse. Sometimes, the trials of life get the better of us and we don't listen for the convictions of the Holy Spirit. In these cases, God will send in others in the body, our friends, to deliver convictions from the Holy Spirit in the form of exhortations. These can be encouragements, admonitions, urgings, corrections, or even recognition of gifts and callings on our lives. These are not prophetic words, but urges from the Holy Spirit to meet conditions so that we can successfully do all that God has called us to. Prophecy often reveals God's predestined will, while the gift of exhortation reveals the conditions of God's predetermined will.

Right now, Jesus is interceding on our behalf so that we will pay attention to the convictions from the Holy Spirit and others in the body in order to receive the increase he wants to give us in our lives. He taught us to pray that the Father's will be done on earth as it is in heaven. If everything that would ever happen has already been predestined by God, then there would be no need for prayer at all. Instead, God has left meeting his conditions up to us in order that his predetermined will might be done on earth, as it is in heaven.

In order to trust God as our Upholder, we will need to learn to lean on convictions and prophecy. Today, there are different types of prophecy. There is prophesying according to our faith, which changes the physical realm around us. There are manifestations of the gift of prophecy which reveal themselves through any believer as the Spirit wills. There is also the gift of the office of the prophet, which is a ministry gift given by Jesus at the time of his ascension. Today, if a prophet is given a word regarding God's predestined times and seasons, he or she should release it so that others in the body can inquire of the Lord to receive convictions revealing what part they may or may not have in the works that come about in those times. When prophecy presents itself, the word should always be weighed by prophets to find out whether or not it is a word that was sent to reveal God's predestined will or his predetermined will. Again, when a revelation of God's predestined will is revealed, signs will always accompany it. When a revelation of his predetermined will is revealed, conditions will accompany it.

God is ready for those who believe in Jesus Christ to trust his position as the upholder so that we remain dependent on him and his spoken Word to stay focused and hopeful as we carry out his will.

14
"I'm ready for my people to trust my perspective."

When I heard God speak those words, I had an idea of what he might have meant, but I also knew that I needed to continue seeking his face for wisdom. As I continued to pray, I looked, and I saw what looked like airplanes flying above the earth. When I saw them, I knew that the perspective we needed would be the perspective from heaven over our situations. Again, I asked for a verse to help me understand how we could learn to trust his perspective. He gave me Philippians 4:2 and Job 22:21-22.

"I entreat Euodia and I entreat Syntyche to agree in the Lord."
Philippians 4:2 ESV

"Agree with God, and be at peace; thereby good will come to

you. Receive instruction from his mouth, and lay up his words in your heart." Job 22:21-22 ESV

When I read the first verse, I wasn't too sure what I was looking at, but then I read the second, I knew that the key to understanding his perspective would be found in the word "agree." This word in the Greek language is "*phroneo,*" and it means "to be of same mind, to cherish the same views, to be harmonious." Looking further into this word, it can also mean "to seek one's interest or advantage, and to be of one's party, siding with him in public affairs."

God is ready for his children to come into unity with him in our minds. We know that by believing in Christ, and being born again, we receive the mind of Christ, but how do we access it? Obviously, if we could look into God's heart, and come into agreement with his mind, we might be able to cherish what he cherishes, and be able to seek out his interests and advantages. We need that! We need to be of one mind with God, so that everything we do will be rooted in our relationship with him and his desires for us and for those he is pursuing. As I continued to study this word, I came upon many more verses throughout the Bible.

"But he turned and said to Peter, "Get behind me, Satan! You are a hindrance to me. For you are not setting your mind on the things of God, but on the things of man." Matthew 16:23 ESV

Chapter 14

This verse should convict every believer to strive to be in one accord with God, cherishing what he values in our hearts. If we ever seek out our own ways, setting our minds on the things of man, we become a hindrance to Christ and to the building up of his kingdom on the earth. Remember, to set our minds on the things of God requires that we first seek him out. When we seek, we find, and when we find, we can set our minds on what we find, coming into agreement with the things of God. I think it is valid to suggest that our minds are battlefields for the warfare being carried out between the kingdom of God and the kingdom of Satan. We know that Satan is not equal to God, he is not his opposite. Yet, if we align ourselves with the things of Satan, man, or this world we live in, we will inevitably oppose God and allow strongholds to be built up within us against Christ.

My wife came to me one day with a revelation that I think applies to this subject. She told me that she had asked God why people continue in sin after coming to know Jesus personally. She said that God told her, "it is because they eat Satan's fruits." If we eat the fruits offered to us by Satan, seeds of his kingdom will be planted on the inside of us, and will eventually bear fruit in our lives. Yet, we are called to resist him and his ways so that he will flee. If we only eat of the fruit of the kingdom of God, we will only bear the fruit of the seeds of the kingdom. Our lives will be full of love, joy, peace, patience, kindness, goodness, faithfulness, gentleness, and self-control. Therefore, I encourage us all to stand firm, having put on the full armor of God that we might extinguish the flaming arrows of the evil one. If we resist the temptations of the enemy, we will not become a hindrance to Christ.

Paul taught us that where sin abounds, grace abounds all the more. Many have read that verse with the understanding that where sin is present in our lives, grace is available to remove the consequences of that sin. However, I believe that this speaking more to the reality of sin being at hand, rather than being in our hearts. If we will learn to resist the temptations to sin, we will receive more grace to keep from sinning. The more we resist sin, the more we will be tempted by the enemy, which means we will require greater measures of grace in our lives to continue resisting. If we want to experience more grace in our lives, we need to resist more sin. Can we live sinless lives? I believe we can, if we will learn to resist temptations to sin. I believe grace will empower us to do just that.

"After three days he called together the local leaders of the Jews, and when they had gathered, he said to them, "Brothers, though I had done nothing against our people or the customs of our fathers, yet I was delivered as a prisoner from Jerusalem into the hands of the Romans. When they had examined me, they wished to set me at liberty, because there was no reason for the

Chapter 14

death penalty in my case. But because the Jews objected, I was compelled to appeal to Caesar—though I had no charge to bring against my nation. For this reason, therefore, I have asked to see you and speak with you, since it is because of the hope of Israel that I am wearing this chain." And they said to him, "We have received no letters from Judea about you, and none of the brothers coming here has reported or spoken any evil about you. But we desire to hear from you what your views are, for with regard to this sect we know that everywhere it is spoken against."

When they had appointed a day for him, they came to him at his lodging in greater numbers. From morning till evening he expounded to them, testifying to the kingdom of God and trying to convince them about Jesus both from the Law of Moses and from the Prophets. And some were convinced by what he said, but others disbelieved. And disagreeing among themselves, they departed after Paul had made one statement: "The Holy Spirit was right in saying to your fathers through Isaiah the prophet:

"'Go to this people, and say, "You will indeed hear but never understand, and you will indeed see but never perceive." For this people's heart has grown dull, and with their ears they can barely hear, and their eyes they have closed; lest they should see with their eyes and hear with their ears and understand with their heart and turn, and I would heal them.'

Therefore let it be known to you that this salvation of God has been sent to the Gentiles; they will listen.

> *He lived there two whole years at his own expense, and welcomed all who came to him, proclaiming the kingdom of God and teaching about the Lord Jesus Christ with all boldness and without hindrance."* Acts 28:17-31 ESV

In these passages, Paul takes a bold opportunity to preach the Gospel to the local leaders of the Jews. It says that when they had appointed a day to hear him speak, they came to him in greater numbers. When they came, he began to testify to his knowledge of the kingdom of God, and he tried to convince all of them about Jesus. Whenever any of us stand in front of people to preach, we do so in hopes that we can convince the people of the things of God and of his Son. To "convince" is to lay out convictions in hopes that people become convinced of them. Paul, therefore, was delivering an exhortation to the people, from a place of personal relationship with the Lord, in order that they might be given an opportunity to know the Lord themselves.

What we need to understand from this passage is that some of them believed what he was saying, and in doing so, they came into agreement with his convictions. Others disagreed with him and did not benefit from his teachings. Paul was not teaching from his own will and desires, but from the convictions the Holy Spirit had placed on him for those people. God was moving through Paul to present convictions through the gift of teaching and exhortation so that these people could come to know Christ personally and receive salvation. The condition that they needed to meet was to agree with the teaching Paul was giving them. For those who were convinced about the kingdom and the Son of God, salvation came with power to heal. However, for those who disagreed with him, their eyes and ears remained closed. They went on from this place spiritually blind and deaf, as the quoted scripture reminds us.

"For those who live according to the flesh set their minds on the things of the flesh, but those who live according to the Spirit set their minds on the things of the Spirit." Romans 8:5 ESV

Our choice to set our minds on the things of the Spirit is synonymous with choosing to live from God's perspective. Every situation we find ourselves in can be viewed by us through the eyes of God. We just need to be willing to seek his perspective for our lives. When people come against us, it's easy to get discouraged and tempted to react defensively. In those times, if we set our minds on the things of the flesh, we will most likely end up retaliating out of anger or self-preservation. Yet, if we seek to understand God's perspective, we can react out of love. It isn't always easy to react in wisdom and maturity, especially when we are under attack verbally or physically, but it is always an option for us. I believe that if we will come into agreement with the character of God, we can endure any situation with clarity, wisdom, and love with the help of the Holy Spirit.

> *"But if some of the branches were broken off, and you, although a wild olive shoot, were grafted in among the others and now share in the nourishing root of the olive tree, do not be arrogant toward the branches. If you are, remember it is not you who support the root, but the root that supports you. Then you will say, "Branches were broken off so that I might be grafted in." That is true. They were broken off because of their unbelief, but you stand fast through faith. So do not become proud, but fear. For if God did not spare the natural branches, neither will he spare you. Note then the kindness and the severity of God: severity toward those who have fallen, but God's kindness to you, provided you continue in his kindness. Otherwise you too will be cut off." Romans 11:17-22 ESV*

It is not us who supports the root, but the root that supports us. This passage is speaking of the relationship between Jews and Gentiles under God, but the principle in the passage regarding the root is applicable to this topic. I think many times Christians pray as though we can convince God to work on our behalf, as if he doesn't already care for us. Even unbelievers pray in their most fearful situations. There's an old saying, "There are no atheists in foxholes." I believe that's true! Whenever people find themselves in situations they can't get out of on their own, the need for God becomes recognized.

Chapter 14

If we ever come to a place in our minds where we think we have come far enough in life that we might be able to handle things on our own, we are mistaken! The need for communion with God is always prevalent regardless of how far we have come in understanding. A branch that does not bear fruit is a branch that is not in agreement with the root, and it should be cut off! However, if we desire to be a branch that bears fruit, we will have to learn to stay in agreement with God and his perspectives.

"May the God of endurance and encouragement grant you to live in such harmony with one another, in accord with Christ Jesus" Romans 15:5 ESV

I believe this verse gives us a key to staying in agreement with other Christians who have received the mind of Christ. We cannot assume that we are capable to abide in him as a community apart from his leading. Therefore, we need to choose to let the God of endurance and encouragement grant us to live in harmony with him, and others. We know that the encouragement we receive from God comes to us by the voice of the Holy Spirit, and the endurance comes through the empowerment of grace granted to us by the quickening spirit of Christ. Relying on God for endurance and empowerment is the only way to remain in harmony and enjoy fellowship with our community of believers.

> *"So if there is any encouragement in Christ, any comfort from love, any participation in the Spirit, any affection and sympathy, complete my joy by being of the same mind, having the same love, being in full accord and of one mind. Do nothing from selfish ambition or conceit, but in humility count others more significant than yourselves. Let each of you look not only to his own interests, but also to the interests of others. Have this mind among yourselves, which is yours in Christ Jesus, who, though he was in the form of God, did not count equality with God a thing to be grasped, but emptied himself, by taking the form of a servant, being born in the likeness of men. And being found in human form, he humbled himself by becoming obedient to the point of death, even death on a cross. Therefore God has highly exalted him and bestowed on him the name that is above every name, so that at the name of Jesus every knee should bow, in heaven and on earth and under the earth, and every tongue confess that Jesus Christ is Lord, to the glory of God the Father."*
> Philippians 2:1-11 ESV

Pride destroys our perspective, and distances us from the help we receive from God to do good works in accordance with his predetermined will. That is why Christ himself became a servant, taking the form of man, and chose to live with a humble and contrite spirit. The most detrimental result of pride in the life of a believer is the absence of prayer. When we don't pray, we become selfish. Prayer is the activity of practicing the presence of God. When we pray, we

Chapter 14

step into God's presence with our own needs and the needs of others in order to seek help from our Provider.

Whenever we attempt to operate in God without keeping with a healthy prayer life, even the work of ministry that may seem appropriate will begin to be rooted in selfish ambition and conceit. We can quickly find ourselves performing religious acts in order to be seen as important. That is not the ministry of Christ, who came not to be served, but to serve. Instead, it is the practice of seeking one's own interests. Remember what was written in Colossians 3 about where our focus should remain as Christians. We are not of this world, but have become ambassadors of the kingdom!

"Set your minds on things that are above, not on things that are on earth." Colossians 3:2 ESV

15
"I'm ready for my people to join me on my vineyard venture."

When God spoke to me about his desire for us to join him on his vineyard venture, it wasn't hard to visualize it. I was taken to a large vineyard in the time of harvest. I saw him picking the best grapes off of each vine. It was like he was on an adventure to find the best fruit produced in the harvest! Again, I asked for a verse, and he gave me 1 Thessalonians 3:11-13 and Colossians 3:12-17.

> *"Now may our God and Father himself, and our Lord Jesus, direct our way to you, and may the Lord make you increase and abound in love for one another and for all, as we do for you, so that he may establish your hearts blameless in holiness before our God and Father, at the coming of our Lord Jesus with all his saints." 1 Thessalonians 3:11-13 ESV*

The two words that were highlighted to me we "increase" and "abound." The Greek word for "increase" is "*pleonazo.*" It means "to super abound and increase in an augmented state." In the context of the vision, this refers to increasing in an augmented production of fruit. The word "abound" in Greek is "*perisseuo,*" which means "exceeding a fixed number of measure, that is to be at hand in abundance, a thing which comes in abundance or overflows unto one in large measure, and again, to overflow."

I believe that God is ready for us to join him on a pursuit for an abundance of good fruit, not only in our own lives but in the lives of others. I believe that we live in the most crucial time in the history of the earth. Overlooking the world, we see sin abounding all the more, but where sin abounds, grace also abounds. We are living in a time when God is pouring our large measures of grace, beyond what we could have even expected or asked for. However, we must be aligned with him, joining ourselves to him in this time to be able to reap the benefits of this ripe field.

Harvest time is short! The time it takes for a farmer to plow the field, sow the seed, water those seeds, and care for the growth is lengthy compared to the time it takes to actually reap the harvest. Whenever the fields have become ripe, the harvest must be taken quickly and without hesitation! One of my pastors was recently ministering in ancient Corinth, and he told me that they were privileged to be present during the time of harvest. He said the grapes were not even comparable to what we buy at the grocery store. In fact, he said that those grapes make ours taste like cardboard! He told me that there is a process during the time that the fruit is becoming ripe where the farmers will test the fruit to gauge the various levels of sugars and other attributes of the fruit to learn when the best time to harvest would be. They do this down to the hour! Whenever the harvest is ready, neighboring farmers and their workers will all come together in the field that is ready and reap it quickly! Then, of course, whenever those neighbor's fields are ready, all will join them in those fields to pick their grapes.

> "After this the Lord appointed seventy-two others and sent them on ahead of him, two by two, into every town and place where he himself was about to go. And he said to them, "The harvest is plentiful, but the laborers are few. Therefore pray earnestly to the Lord of the harvest to send out laborers into his harvest." Luke 10:1-2 ESV

From the story that my pastor shared with me, and the words of the above verse, I came to the conclusion that there are not enough laborers because there are not enough true neighbors to help reap the harvest. The fields are ready, but there are not enough laborers! If the fields are not picked in time, within a matter of hours, the grapes can quickly spoil. Looking at our world today, I would say that there are many "spoiled" grapes that have not been hand-picked for the kingdom of God! When God searches for the best fruits, he is searching for those who do not yet know him! I believe God is going to allow his church, if we will remain obedient to his Word and to the leading of the Spirit, to reap a massive harvest of souls. For this to take place, we will need to become better neighbors.

I live in the "Bible-belt" area of the United States. There are around three hundred churches in our region alone, in a population of somewhere around four hundred-thousand people. Although these church congregations are meeting, they are not all in unity. I do not know the names of all of these churches and gatherings, and I don't know the people who lead them personally. That in itself limits my own ability to come into unity with them on issues within the community. The only way that all of these churches could come into unity with each other is through the Spirit.

Unity in the Spirit allows us to function independently while also functioning as one whole body. If all of the leaders of all of these church gatherings become attentive to the voice of the Holy Spirit, we could begin to reap a harvest of souls together for the kingdom of God. It wouldn't take long at all to see our cities change. This is why we can all come together in one field, all over the world, to reap a harvest that is plentiful. How do we do that? How can we know if we are in unity with God and others?

I think in order for us to ever come into true unity, we will need to recognize not only the need to become better neighbors with other churches and communities, but to also recognize the need to become better ministers. Looking at a similar passage in Matthew, we see another perspective of labor.

> *"And Jesus went throughout all the cities and villages, teaching in their synagogues and proclaiming the gospel of the kingdom and healing every disease and every affliction. When he saw the crowds, he had compassion for them, because they were harassed and helpless, like sheep without a shepherd. Then he said to his disciples, "The harvest is plentiful, but the laborers are few; therefore pray earnestly to the Lord of the harvest to send out laborers into his harvest." Matthew 9:35-38 ESV*

Here, we see things taken a bit further. Previously, I had recognized the need to become better neighbors. While that's true, let's dig into the context of Christ's words here in Matthew. Here, it says that after he had been teaching in their synagogues and proclaiming the Gospel, healing the sick and every affliction, he still saw a people in need of a shepherd. It was for this reason (the need for a shepherd), that he gave the command to pray earnestly for laborers. In this context, I see the need for pastors. I believe Jesus was seeing the need for more pastors in these communities. Whenever we are praying for more laborers, I believe we need to not only pray that we should become better neighbors, but also that we should not neglect the need to be pastored, and the need to equip more pastors to shepherd the sheep of the nations.

"Put on then, as God's chosen ones, holy and beloved, compassionate hearts, kindness, humility, meekness, and patience, bearing with one another and, if one has a complaint against another, forgiving each other; as the Lord has forgiven you, so you also must forgive. And above all these put on love, which binds everything together in perfect harmony. And let the peace of Christ rule in your hearts, to which indeed you were called in one body. And be thankful. Let the word of Christ dwell in you richly, teaching and admonishing one another in all wisdom, singing psalms and hymns and spiritual songs, with thankfulness in your hearts to God. And whatever you do, in word or deed, do everything in the name of the Lord Jesus, giving thanks to God the Father through him." Colossians 3:12-17 ESV

The conditions given in the above verse, if obeyed, bring the church into unity. If we will seek first to put on love, we will be bound together in perfect harmony. Then, and only then, can the peace of Christ rule in power within all of our hearts, which is what we have been called to in one body! Unfortunately, not all who call themselves Christians live in personal relationship with Jesus, or are led by the Spirit. Not all who call themselves Christians put on compassionate hearts, kindness, meekness, and patience. Not all who call themselves Christians have truly entered a spiritual lifestyle that requires full surrender to the Lord Jesus, and complete forgiveness toward each other and others. Yet, if we will seek to love, obeying the two great commands, we will come into unity through that love.

God is ready for us to stop living in unforgiveness. If we will meet that condition, the Spirit of God will invite us to join him on his vineyard venture. He will give us important revelation regarding the people who are ripe and ready for harvest. He will send us in, together, to reap a harvest of souls, and to make disciples of nations. The Great Commission has not yet been fulfilled. Right now, there are still unreached people groups around the world. Some of these nations and groups are ripe for harvest, but we must become dependent on the voice of the Spirit in order to be led into those fields with power to preach the Gospel and make disciples. These people are the fruit God desires. Not only unreached people groups around the world, but the unreached people in our own cities and regions who have never come to know him personally.

Trusting God's position as the upholder will instill the necessity for rest into our lives. This is where we will receive total spiritual, soulical, and physical rest, being revived to maintain fruitful ministries.

Trusting God's perspective will help us to become reliant on daily bread, that daily word from God. By seeking the things that are above, coming into agreement with those things, and setting our hearts and minds on them, we will come into agreement with God's good plans.

By preparing ourselves in these ways, I believe we will become fully aware of the opportunities we have all around us to shepherd our communities as loving neighbors, ready to do the work of the Father, as he wills and as he leads. By following his lead, we will bear abundant fruit among the nations!

16
Laying Down Sin

Continuing with the topic of conviction, I want to point out its power to help lead us into living a life without sin. Many people view the idea of convictions through a negative lens, as if they come to us in the form of condemnation, but that isn't the purpose of conviction. In fact, they never work to cause us to feel any form of condemnation. The Holy Spirit is not the accuser, but the Comforter. He is the Advocate and Helper of the children of God. He always points us toward a more comforting position in God by revealing our true callings and identities through convictions. To begin, I want us to look at how the voice of the Holy Spirit works in our lives to lead us into sonship.

> *"And have you forgotten the exhortation that addresses you as sons? 'My son, do not regard lightly the discipline of the Lord, nor be weary when reproved by him. For the Lord disciplines the one he loves, and chastises every son whom he receives.'"* Hebrews 12:5-6 ESV

Remember, the Holy Spirit is not only a Teacher, Helper, Comforter, and Counselor, but he is also a Parent. Parents are called to discipline their children in a loving way, seeing to it that they are raised up in the way that they should walk. Would God teach us to raise our children up in the way they should go if he does not do the same himself? No, God is not double-minded, but perfect in all his ways. Therefore, it is in his nature as a Father, through the teachings of Christ, and the voice of the Holy Spirit, to discipline us as sons and daughters in the kingdom.

Whenever we receive any form of discipline from God, it is not for the purpose of condemnation, but for training in righteousness. The word "discipline" in these verses defines the whole training and education of children (in relations to the cultivation of the mind and morals), through commands, admonitions, reproof, and punishment. It also includes training in regards to caring for our physical bodies. This type of discipline is directed toward the souls of God's children, and presents itself through the convictions of the Holy Spirit in order to correct mistakes and curb passions. It is for the purpose of increasing virtue in our souls, in order to bring to fruition a more full and mature perfection of our soulish nature in Christ Jesus.

These verses give us a few keys as to how the discipline of the Spirit is received. They mention reproof and chastisement to be those processes in which we are guided into maturity. Reproof is literally defined, "to convict, refute, or confute, generally in order to bring to the light and expose that which is detrimental to the mind. To find fault with, or correct by word in order to reprehend severely, chide, admonish, or reprove, calling to account some fault, and demanding an explanation."

With this understanding in mind, we need to realize that the reproofing discipline from the Holy Spirit calls to account what is leading us away from his purposes for our lives. It exposes the darkness with light in order to bring us into a realization of its inconsistency with our nature and the knowledge of God. One typical question I get asked is, "How will I know the difference between God's voice of conviction and the enemy's voice of condemnation?" One of my leaders answers in one of the simplest, but most powerful ways. He says, "If the voice brings you closer to God, it's God, but if it pushes you further away, it's the enemy!"

Whenever the Holy Spirit reproves us, we must be willing to give him an explanation for the thoughts and intentions of our hearts. When we do, we will instantly realize what needs to be done, because we will be in acknowledgment of our thinking's inability to meet our needs in the way that God desires to. He never wants us to be led into darkness, but instead desires that we listen to the voice of the Spirit, even when it is disciplinary, so that we can receive the provisions he wants to pour out in our lives.

Abiding in Christ is an impossible task without the help of the Holy Spirit! If we ever choose to neglect his voice, we grieve him! The Holy Spirit has not come to be grieved, rejected, or neglected, but to be heard. When he fell on the people in the upper room in Acts 2, he came with the power of his speech, and immediately began revealing the truth about the time and season that had come into fruition on the earth. Still today, he speaks to the children of God in order to accomplish what the Father sent him to do.

Another key to understanding the disciplinary speech of the Holy Spirit is chastisement. This is a harsher form of punishment from God, which indeed takes place in the lives of those who neglect to obey his words. It literally means "to scourge," which describes the scourging of a whip, plague, calamity, or misfortune sent by God in order to punish disobedience. We see this best explained in the fact that God allowed a spirit of stupor to rest on the children of disobedience in the wilderness. He did this as a result of their unwillingness to heed his words, and it kept many from entering into the Promised Land, even Moses. God did not do this because he did not love Moses as his own child, but for the purpose of showing discipline to the ones he truly loved.

Even today, many of the Jews do not understand the mysteries of the kingdom, for their eyes have not been opened to the truth. This too is an ongoing representation of God's chastisement for disobedience. It isn't that God has not already revealed his plan for the salvation of his people, but the opposite! He unfolded it through the prophetic word and through many events that were fulfilled by Christ when he sent his own Son into the world to fulfill those prophecies. If the Jewish people will seek the Scriptures for what they reveal, he would open their eyes to the fact that Jesus is the Messiah, but until they do, he chastises them with the ongoing hindrance of this spirit of stupor in order that they may endure the discipline of their disobedience having both their spiritual eyes and ears closed off to the truth.

"What then? Israel failed to obtain what it was seeking. The elect obtained it, but the rest were hardened, as it is written, 'God gave them a spirit of stupor, eyes that would not see and ears that would not hear, down to this very day.' And David says, 'Let their table become a snare and a trap, a stumbling block

and a retribution for them; let their eyes be darkened so that they cannot see, and bend their backs forever.' So I ask, did they stumble that they might fall? By no means! Rather through their trespass salvation has come to the Gentiles, so as to make Israel jealous." Romans 11:7-11 ESV

Again, it was not that God did not love the Israelites that he gave them this spirit of stupor, but rather because he did love them that he disciplined them. If he did not deal with them justly, would there be a need for a Savior who came to the earth and lived a sinless life? No! Yet, because God is just in his own nature, he deals justly with his own people who are called by his name, therefore disobedience and lawlessness had to be dealt with justly through his Son Jesus, who came to fulfill the Law and declare liberty to the captives. Now that the Gospel message has been fully walked out in Christ's sinless and obedient life, death, burial, and resurrection, justice is available to all who will believe in him. We live in a time that is quickly coming to a close, in which we can all willingly choose to believe in him. Soon, he will return on the clouds and every knee will bow and every tongue will confess that he is Lord, both in heaven and on the earth.

"It is for discipline that you have to endure. God is treating you as sons. For what son is there whom his father does not discipline? If you are left without discipline, in which all have participated, then you are illegitimate children and not sons.

Chapter 16

Besides this, we have had earthly fathers who disciplined us and we respected them. Shall we not much more be subject to the Father of spirits and live? For they were disciplined for a short time as it seemed best to them, but he disciplines us for our good, that we may share in his holiness. For the moment all discipline seems painful rather than pleasant, but later it yields the peaceful fruit of righteousness to those who have been trained by it." Hebrews 12:7-11 ESV

Another purpose for the convictions of the Holy Spirit is to prepare us to take dominion with Christ over all things, even now, by cooperating with him in the Spirit.

"Those whom I love, I reprove and discipline, so be zealous and repent. Behold, I stand at the door and knock. If anyone hears my voice and opens the door, I will come in to him and eat with him, and he with me. The one who conquers, I will grant him to sit with me on my throne, as I also conquered and sat down with my Father on his throne." Revelation 3:19-21 ESV

This set of scriptures is an exhortation from Christ himself, revealing both conditions and provisions. The conditions we need to meet are that of becoming zealous and of repenting. If we will meet those conditions, we will be given dominion with Christ, to rule with him having obtained dominion through relationship.

To be zealous is to be jealous, but not in an unholy way. It comes from a Greek word, "*zelos*," which describes the excitement of the mind or fervor of the spirit toward something. It is the embracing, pursuing, or defending of anything on behalf of a person or thing with fierceness of indignation. That word comes from its root, "*zeo*," which means "to boil with heat, whether that is the heat of righteous anger or love, again, being fervent in spirit for what is good." In Revelation 3:15-16, Jesus says:

> *"I know your works: you are neither cold nor hot. Would that you were either cold or hot! So, because you are lukewarm, and neither hot nor cold, I will spit you out of my mouth." Revelation 3:15-16 ESV*

I believe the purpose for this example of "cold and hot" is derived from the necessity for zeal in Christian life. We definitely don't want to be cold! We should earnestly desire to pursue Christ with a righteous zeal from the Holy Spirit, so that we become defenders of his name all over the earth! Even before we came to know the Lord, the Holy Spirit spoke to us in order to lead us into a righteous zeal for the Lord. We may have though that all was well in our lives because we had no knowledge of truth. Yet, the Holy Spirit made it clear to us, even when we were sinners, that we were in desperate need of something more than ourselves. He did so through the power of conviction.

Chapter 16

The other condition provided here is that of repentance. Like convictions, the need for repentance is usually viewed through a negative lens, as it has been taught throughout past generations as a religious necessity rather than a provision of forgiveness. Because of this, many people understand repentance as a recognition of sin and a turning away from it. That is not what repentance is! That is the result of true repentance, but it is not the process for receiving repentance.

Repentance is a grant from the Father, not a loan. It is something freely given, not something borrowed. Therefore, our willingness to repent is only as applicable to our lives as our acknowledgment of the need for forgiveness. When we recognize any need for forgiveness in our lives, we should seek the Lord zealously for a complete change in our hearts, which will lead to a complete transformation of our minds, and finally, a change in action. Turning away from sin, therefore, is the result of true repentance, but not the process. If any of us fall away from God in some form of disobedience, this free gift of repentance is always available to us as long as we are willing to meet the condition of acknowledging the sin and the necessity for a complete change of heart, mind, and action. True repentance is embracing a transformation from carnal nature into spiritual fervor.

"Nevertheless, I tell you the truth: it is to your advantage

that I go away, for if I do not go away, the Helper will not come to you. But if I go, I will send him to you. And when he comes, he will convict the world concerning sin and righteousness and judgement: concerning sin, because they do not believe in me; concerning righteousness, because I go to the Father, and you will see me no longer; concerning judgement, because the ruler of this world is judged." John 16:7-11 ESV

Along with convicting us to live sinless lives as sons and daughters of God, and living up to the conditions of zeal and repentance, the Holy Spirit also convicts us in order to increase faith, righteousness, and authority. This began before we ever entered into a relationship with Jesus, but carries on as we are learning to develop healthy spiritual lifestyles.

When the Holy Spirit convicts the world of sin, it is because of the presence of unbelief. Obviously, he is working to expose the unbelief in order to reveal the opportunity to enter into faith. Whenever someone of the world enters into faith, those convictions do not stop flowing from the Spirit. He will continually convict us of any unbelief in our lives in order that we might be able to enter into greater levels of faith. Whether that is the initial faith that we have in Jesus, or if it is faith for manifestational gifts of the Spirit that come in spontaneous moments as he wills, the Holy Spirit himself helps us to believe for more. Where there is more faith, there is less sin,

Chapter 16

and where there is less sin, there is more power. If we want to live abundant lives and experience more of the power of God at work in us, we will need more faith.

He also convicts of righteousness because we do not see Jesus any longer in the flesh. By convicting us of righteousness, the Holy Spirit is actually teaching us how to follow Christ as if he were still on the earth. If we will learn to listen to these convictions, we can experience the same type of training that Jesus gave the disciples, answering their questions and counseling them toward holiness. We do have the Word of God, which helps us to see how Jesus taught the disciples to live, but because we also have the presence of the promised Holy Spirit, we can experience the same teaching more personally through his spoken word. Remember that Jesus only spoke as he heard the Father speak. The Holy Spirit operates in the same way. Therefore, the disciples were trained up by the Father in heaven, and through the Holy Spirit, we too are trained up in righteousness by the Father himself. From the time we lived in the world, chasing the passions of our former ignorance until now, the Holy Spirit has been guiding us into righteousness as the Father gives him utterance.

> *"As for those who persist in sin, rebuke them in the presence of all, so that the rest may stand in fear. In the presence of God and of Christ Jesus and of the elect angels I charge you to keep*

these rules without prejudging, doing nothing from partiality" 1 Timothy 5:20-21 ESV

Finally, in order to help the body of Christ learn to lay down sin and take up holiness, the Holy Spirit speaks through ministers in order to deliver convictions to those who will not receive them internally by the Spirit himself. This form of convictions is aimed toward careful obedience in leadership. Not given so that men may lord over other men, but that we might, by pursuing love, lead the body of Christ into full maturity in the stature of Christ. This is never to be carried out under a demonic spiritual prejudice, or through partiality to any particular people, but instead, it is to be carried out in love. If this type of correction is administered through a leader in a church gathering, let the leader demonstrate matured repentance on behalf of the elect as well, as we are one body. If the leader is the one being corrected, let the leader demonstrate a process of true repentance before being allowed back into a continued ministry role. Again, this must never be done out of partiality or prejudice, but in love for the sake of accountability.

17
Confirming God's Presence

The greatest reality we are privileged to embrace since the outpouring of the Holy Spirit in Acts 2 is God's presence. His presence has always been around, but not in the way that we can experience it since that day. In the Old Testament, there are many examples of the presence of God, but all of them happened in order to fulfill a specific purpose at a specific time in one's life. In these last days, God has poured his Spirit out on all flesh in order that we might all be given the opportunity to live by and practice knowing the powerful presence of the Almighty God. Of course, not all who live on the earth today have received the baptism of the Holy Spirit, or even the seal of the Holy Spirit that occurs at the time of spiritual birth into eternal life.

> *"In the beginning, God created the heavens and the earth. The earth was without form and void, and darkness was over the face of the deep. And the Spirit of God was hovering over the face of the waters." Genesis 1:1-2 ESV*

In these two verses, we see that the darkness was present over the face of the deep, and that the Spirit hovered over the face of the waters. Even before the earth was formed, the Spirit was moving. The word "hovering" in Hebrew describes movement. As for the darkness, there is no implication of movement. Therefore, the darkness was present over the face of the deep, which refers to the abyss and the deep parts of the sea, and the Spirit hovered and moved over the face of the waters. Another word for that is often used in place of "hovering" is "brooding."

When a mother hen rests on top of her eggs, that is called brooding. I use this example to help us get a picture of the nurturing movement of the Spirit. Not only does this word imply movement in the Hebrew language, but it also describes "watchful care." When the Holy Spirit was poured out on all flesh in Acts 2, the same type of movement occurred. To put it into perspective as to how people react to his movement, we will continue with the idea of a hen brooding over her eggs. Although the Spirit has been poured out on all flesh, not all flesh has received the seed by which they become germinated to be born again, receiving life. The eggs we buy at the grocery store have not been fertilized by a seed, and do not have any chicks growing in them in an embryonic state. The same is true for all flesh. Some of us have received the seed, that is, the Gospel, which is to be accepted and received in order to provide power for entering into eternal life.

Therefore, although the Spirit has been poured out on all flesh, until any person living in a body of flesh receives the seed of Christ by accepting the Gospel and applying faith to their reception of knowledge, they do not receive eternal life. Instead, they are like unfertilized eggs that will never be made alive. We who have received eternal life have been made alive with Christ and have received the Spirit by whom we cry "Abba! Father!" (Romans 8:15, Galatians 4:6). When that occurs, through the Spirit of adoption we become sons and daughters of God, who are privileged to embrace a relationship with the presence of the Holy Spirit while on the earth, even before we receive our spiritual, glorified bodies. Because we become hosts of the presence of the Spirit of God, we can be convicted in ways that confirm his presence in the midst of our struggles. Not only does he speak to us through the Spirit, but he also cares for us in our unknowing, watching over us and keeping us until we enter into the fulness of eternal life through a process of resurrection on the last day.

As we learned in the previous chapter, God disciplines us through the convictions of the Spirit, not because he enjoys punishment, but because he loves us.

"Those whom I love, I reprove and discipline, so be zealous and repent." Revelation 3:19 ESV

We receive convictions because we are valuable to God. Our value is not in our works, but in the sacrifice of his Son. The cross of Christ is not a revelation of our unworthiness or of our sin, but it is a revelation of our value. Whenever the Holy Spirit speaks to us concerning any aspect of life where we may be falling away, he does so in order to remind us of the price that was paid for us on the cross. God allowed his only begotten Son, through whom all things in heaven and on earth were created, to be crucified on a cross, endure the grave, and experience resurrection life in order that we might understand the love that he has for us. He not only loves us, but he also paid an incalculable ransom for our souls so that we might be joined with him forever in eternal glory.

18
Conviction in Fellowship

"If your brother sins against you, go and tell him his fault, between you and him alone. If he listens to you, you have gained your brother. But if he does not listen, take one or two others along with you, that every charge may be established by the evidence of two or three witnesses. If he refuses to listen to them, tell it to the church. And if he refuses to listen even to the church, let him be to you as a Gentile and a tax collector. Truly I say to you, whatever you bind on earth shall be bound in heaven, and whatever you loose on earth shall be loosed in heaven. Again I say to you, if two of you agree on earth about anything they ask, it will be done for them by my Father in heaven. For where two or three are gathered in my name, there I am among them."
Matthew 18:15-20 ESV

This passage is all about how to embrace those we fellowship with whenever they sin against us. What we need to learn from this is that it is not ok to ignore the reality of sin within the fellowship of Christians. Unfortunately, we are not all perfect. The presence of God is among us, working to bring us into perfection, but we will experience what it feels like for brothers and sisters to sin against us in the process. Whenever that happens, we need to be willing to bring that out into the open, respectfully and in love, so that the person may be reminded of the necessity to acknowledge that sin so that the relationship between the members of the body is restored in love. In the same way, we must never neglect any opportunity to seek the forgiveness of others when we sin against them. If another brother or sister approaches us with evidence of any way that we might have sinned against them, we need to address it.

This is another form of conviction. Whenever we expose sin within the body of Christ, the love of Christ can work to extinguish it. What we need to understand is that any conviction we receive from another Christian does not come to us in order to bring shame, guilt, or condemnation. Instead, they come because we are sought for favor and fellowship. God expects us to learn to live in harmony with one another, experiencing life together in love. Whenever a body is in unity, clear of any sins against one another, the atmosphere of fellowship creates room for us to favor one another in honor and respect for the gift each one of us is to the body of Christ.

> *"For there are many who are insubordinate, empty talkers and deceivers, especially those of the circumcision party. They must be silenced, since they are upsetting whole families by teaching for shameful gain what they ought not teach. One of the Cretans, a prophet of their own, said, 'Cretans are always liars, evil beasts, lazy gluttons.' This testimony is true. Therefore rebuke them sharply, that they may be sound in the faith, not devoting themselves to Jewish myths and the commands of people who turn away from the truth. To the pure, all things are pure, but to the defiled and unbelieving, nothing is pure; but both their minds and their consciences are defiled. They profess to know God, but they deny him by their works. They are detestable, disobedient, unfit for any good work."* Titus 1:10-ESV

19
Soundness of Faith

We have been chosen for soundness of faith. That means that whenever we minister to others, we should always be rooted in faith. We have not been commissioned to carry out a ministry of religion, but of love. Therefore, whenever we seek to counsel or instruct others in the body, we should do so out of love for God and faith in Christ. He is the hope of glory! If hope does not accompany our message, we are not in alignment with Christ. Whenever teachings are being performed out of a lack of faith, it disrupts the progress of the kingdom and distances us from the goodness of God. We should not teach based off of the doctrines of man, but from our personal relationship with the Holy Spirit, who in himself contains righteousness, joy, and peace.

"If you love me, you will keep my commandments. And I will ask the Father, and he will give you another Helper, to be with you forever, even the Spirit of truth, whom the world cannot receive, because it neither sees him nor knows him. You know him, for he dwells with you and will be in you.

I will not leave you as orphans; I will come to you. Yet a little while and the world will see me no more, but you will see me. Because I live, you will also live. In that day you will know that I am in my father, and you in me, and I in you. Whoever has my commandments and keeps them, he it is who loves me. And he who loves me will be loved by my Father, and I will love him and manifest myself to him. Judas (not Iscariot) said to him, Lord, how is it that you will manifest yourself to us, and not to the world? Jesus answered him, "If anyone loves me, he will keep my word, and my Father will love him, and we will come to him and make our home with him. Whoever does not love me does not keep my words. And the word that you hear is not mine but the Father's who sent me.

These things I have spoken with you while I am still with you. But the Helper, the Holy Spirit, whom the Father will send in my name, he will teach you all things and bring to remembrance all that I have said to you. Peace I leave with you, my peace I give to you. Not as the world gives do I give to you. Let not your hearts be troubled, neither let them be afraid. You heard me say to you, I am going away, and I will come to you. If you loved me, you would have rejoiced, because I am going to the Father, for the

Chapter 19

Father is greater than I. And now I have told you before it takes place, so that when it does take place you will believe. I will no longer talk much with you, for the ruler of this world is coming. He has no claim on me, but I do as the Father has commanded me, so that the world may know that I love the Father. Rise, let us go from here." John 14:15-31 ESV

One perspective to consider regarding how the convictions of the Holy Spirit confirm God's presence in our daily lives is that he has come to help us, comfort us, teach us, and remind us. Sometimes convictions remind us of what we have already learned, but have neglected to walk out. Other times, they may reveal new aspects of Christ's character that we need to understand in order to more maturely walk in his identity.

If we don't love Jesus, there would be no desire within us to obey his commandments. However, if we do love him, and are passionate in pursuing his manifested identity in our own lives, we will seek and strive to be obedient to them. By simply hearing of the Gospel, but never knowing Jesus personally, obedience to his commandments might seem religious. In effect, the desire to obey him is actually rooted in a mental bondage to slavery, rather than in a love for relationship with a personal Savior. When we begin to live out an intimate love relationship with the Lord, we not only seek to know him more, but we also strive to obey him, again, not as a result of religious bondage, but as a result of unconditional love for his presence.

If we obey him, the Word says that he will ask the Father and the Father will send the Spirit to begin a work in our lives of deep personal conviction. One of the first commandments we are told to follow is baptism. Most of us understand that water baptism is an outward profession of faith in Christ, but it is also a fulfillment of a command of Jesus. It is not the only command worthy of following in order to receive the Spirit, which is why some received him before water baptism, but it is a commandment that, if followed, reveals our willingness to be obedient to the commands of Christ as a result of a love for him.

Water baptism is usually one of the first things we do as Christians in regard to outward public professions of faith. Just as the Ethiopian eunuch was baptized by Phillip immediately following his reception of the Gospel message. I don't think this is a religious practice, but a basic physical command that helps new believers understand the importance of cleansing and regeneration in Christ. I know many who, before baptism, were confused about their faith, but who after baptism, began to hear the voice of the Holy Spirit in a brand-new way. Instead of convictions of sin, righteousness, and judgment, the convictions began to come to them for the purpose of help, comfort, and guidance.

Chapter 19

This shift in our personal relationship with the Holy Spirit happens when we die to our old selves and are raised to newness of life in the Spirit and in the kingdom. Those who belong to the kingdom of God do not belong to the world, but to the Spirit. We have been born again, not of the flesh, but of the Spirit, that we might have hope for resurrection, a taste of the heavenly provision given through the deposit and seal of the Holy Spirit.

God's desire to keep us in his will by manifesting his Son to us through the Holy Spirit in order that he might come and dwell in us, by faith generates peace. That peace of God works to sustain us in love, life, and in the Spirit, in order that our hearts not grow hardened, faint, or troubled in this life. Instead, we are more than conquerors through Christ. Our hearts remain convicted that we might become holy. As we strive to remain in Christ, we should lean on the voice of the Spirit who teaches us all things.

Therefore, rejoice! By the Spirit of God we are able to allow God to uphold us with his perspective, and by making his home in us, allows us to bear fruit, plant seeds, and reap bountiful harvests. God has not chosen to leave us on the earth without his presence, but has chosen to send the Spirit so that we can live effectively both inwardly and outwardly for Christ. With hearts convicted, we become holy, like God, bearing his image and likeness for all the world to see, so that they too might know the perfect peace and presence of our God.

www.ingramcontent.com/pod-product-compliance
Lightning Source LLC
Chambersburg PA
CBHW061320040426
42444CB00011B/2716